THE WHALE AND THE CUPCAKE

D0051265

The Whale & the Cupcake

STORIES OF SUBSISTENCE, LONGING, AND COMMUNITY IN ALASKA

Julia O'Malley

FOREWORD BY KIM SEVERSON

ANCHORAGE MUSEUM
Anchorage

UNIVERSITY OF WASHINGTON PRESS
Seattle

CONTENTS

FOREWORD

KIM SEVERSON

The belly of a wild Alaska salmon is a delicious secret. Too often, someone lucky enough to have a fat, fresh salmon in their possession will pass over the belly in favor of a thick filet. It's a shame, really.

One summer not too long ago, I had some of those beautiful bellies sizzling on a sheet pan in a friend's cabin on Kachemak Bay. My friend and her neighbors who live in Halibut Cove know the value of those bellies, so when they came together to process their collective catch earlier that summer they were careful to slice them into perfect chunks and then transform them with smoke.

I stared out at the water where those very fish had been running strong only a few weeks earlier and stirred a pot of Carolina white corn grits I had carried to Alaska in my suitcase from Atlanta, where I live now.

My idea was to create a cousin of shrimp and grits, the dish that sustained people who fished the waters in the South Carolina Lowcountry for centuries, using the fish that has sustained the people who have lived in Alaska for much longer. And then, that evening, I would feed my creation to Julia O'Malley, whose book you hold in your hands.

I tell you this story because this book reminded me of that meal and of several others she and I have shared across the years. It's a book about connection and adaptation, about tradition and the very human need we have to feed each other. Like this book, cooking tells us where we have been, where we are, and where we are going.

Julia, a daughter of Alaska, has taken her place in a long line of people who have chronicled the ways in which food sustains and defines the state's culture. Many people have written Alaska cookbooks or labored over academic studies on subsistence. But there has never been a book that explores what it means to eat in Alaska with such intimacy and breadth.

Julia examines Alaska's kitchens, farm fields, and supply chains with the skills of a reporter and the heart of a cook. She explains the importance of a sea lion meatball, the pleasures in a can of evaporated milk, and how the evolution of hoop houses transformed the state's short, glorious growing season to the cheers of everyone who has paid six dollars for a head of browning lettuce.

I first met Julia when she walked into the newsroom of the *Anchorage Daily News*. I was an editor whose tasks included writing about the state's restaurants. I watched her grow up and leave for college in the Northeast, then return to build her family and craft her career as journalist.

I left, too, for newspaper work that allowed me to spend the better part of the last twenty years chronicling the way America eats, from the organic salad plates of San Francisco to the high-velocity kitchens of New York to the African roots of a southern Sunday supper. But Alaska, where practicality and adaptation run alongside an ever-present sense of longing and loyalty, is where I really learned about how important food is to a community.

Sure, Californians might love the avocado they picked from a backyard tree the way Texans love their barbecue or New Yorkers celebrate apple cider in the fall, but that love cannot compare to Alaskan food sacraments like picking blueberries from a mountainside, carrying a bowl of moose broth to a family member stuck in the Alaska Native Hospital, or having a whole king eider sea duck in the freezer.

It is a rare Alaskan—a newcomer, probably—who doesn't need to taste the wild food of the state regularly. But about 95 percent of Alaska's food is shipped in from somewhere else, and that creates a unique pantry.

Julia is a fan of that pantry. She devotes a whole chapter to explaining why store-bought cake mixes in the most remote villages matter almost as much as whale meat, and another digging into why Costcos in Alaska have to stock pilot bread and Tang.

She also gets at the longing that hangs over the Alaska kitchen. When I wrote a restaurant column for the *Anchorage Daily News*, I ran an annual contest asking readers to vote for one type of restaurant they wished would open. I figured people might ask for dim sum or shawarma—global dishes that were shaping the culinary landscape in other American cities but had yet to reach Anchorage.

Invariably, people voted for Red Lobster even though they live in a place where the sweetest shrimp I have ever tasted and fresh king crab legs as big as batons are there for the taking. The vote was not about the seafood, but about a longing to be part of the American culture they saw on TV. This feeling is part of, as Julia writes, "a rub between self-reliance and longing, a dissonance at the center of the Alaskan experience."

And did I mention there are recipes? Julia studied every old Alaska cookbook she could find and then took to her own kitchen to offer clear-eyed renditions of some of the state's greatest hits, like salmon pot pie and Halibut Olympia.

But there are modern takes, too, like gluten-free versions of sourdough pancakes and precise instructions for building a classic Alaska cocktail using gin from some of the state's new distilleries.

Make one and toast the work you find in these pages. It is a gift.

∾

KIM SEVERSON is a Pulitzer Prize–winning food correspondent for the *New York Times*. Previously she served as news and features editor and reporter at the *Anchorage Daily News*. A four-time James Beard Award recipient for food writing, she is the author of four books, including *Spoon Fed: How Eight Cooks Saved My Life*.

THE WHALE AND THE CUPCAKE

Introduction

What Why How We Eat

There's a corner parking lot outside what used to be the Sears store in Anchorage that has been an unofficial marketplace as long as I can remember. Sometimes its merchants have traveled in from villages to sell ivory carvings or pieces of bowhead baleen—ebony ridges from the mouth of a whale, long as a roof beam. Mostly, though, it's food. Shrimp pulled from the ice-cold waters of the Gulf of Alaska, fresh eggs in wintertime, or king crab legs advertised with a crooked sign.

When I was a kid, every summer we'd find a man there who brought cases of peaches in from somewhere down south. I had been used to the hard grocery store peaches that ripen in dark container ships on their way to Anchorage. By contrast, the fragrance and texture of those parking lot peaches bloomed in my mouth. I ate till my tongue went raw. My mom sliced them for the freezer, her mind on January's darkness. For years, on that corner, there were also doughnuts, always Krispy Kremes, rumpled boxes piled high on a card table, carried up from Seattle, not fresh or hot but still somehow precious, carrying the worldly mystery of Outside.

The story of Alaska's relationship with food might be told on that corner. With every generation, Alaska grows more diverse and connects farther to the outside world, but there are ways in which we will never be able to transcend the distance, physical and psychological. What Alaskans eat is an amalgam of

There is most likely no more democratic fishing spot in America than Kenai, Alaska. It's a place where any Alaskan, from an oil company executive to a car wash attendant, can fish free during a three-week stretch in July.

wild-sourced foods, intricately tied to our landscape and identity, and foods that travel wildly long distances to get here from faraway homes we long for or places we can only imagine. And that reflects a rub between self-reliance and longing, a dissonance at the center of the Alaskan experience.

I've been a cater-waiter and a prep cook. I've worked behind a cheese counter and at an espresso machine. I came to writing about Alaska's food culture after years of covering Anchorage's ethnic and immigrant communities for the *Anchorage Daily News*. Immigration shaped Anchorage into one of the most diverse cities in the country, and as I wrote about Lao Buddhist monks, Korean entrepreneurs, Hmong animists, and Pacific Islander youth, I kept finding myself in kitchens, behind barbecue grills, in tiny grocery stores, and at community gatherings with long potluck tables.

Food became my ticket in. When subjects were difficult and complicated, asking about what was on the table or in the pot put people at ease. Eating what people cooked for me built trust and piqued my curiosity.

When I left full-time work at the paper to care for my youngest son in 2014, I began freelancing for national publications. The first essay I wrote during that period, for the food website Eater, was about a cousin who raises pigs in Homer. My editor, Helen Rosner, asked me, "What is Alaska cuisine?" That question has remained in the back of my head ever since. This collection of writings, recipes, and interviews, and the Anchorage Museum exhibit that accompanies it, seek to begin a conversation that might answer the question.

I've made one conclusion: True Alaska cuisine is most often found in home kitchens and community gathering places, not restaurants. Alaskans, many who are from somewhere else, are well traveled and spend a lot of time thinking about food. Lots of everyday people here are experts at wild food processing, which is another thing that sets our food culture apart. The most innovative and delicious dishes I've eaten—things like par-smoked black cod, crispy-skinned anise-scented local pork, a sourdough boule, and crab apple jelly—are at kitchen tables.

And another observance, there is often cultural contrast at the center of our plates: Twinkies and rice steamed in banana leaves at a Buddhist temple in Anchorage, Betty Crocker Cake Mix cupcakes and fermented whale in Point Hope on the arctic coast, and smoked salmon eggs and Filipino-style spiced mango on the Instagram feed of a Juneau chef.

Shortly after the Eater essay was published, I began work on a project with photographer Katie Orlinsky, funded by the Pulitzer Center for Crisis Reporting, which examined the intersection of climate change and subsistence hunting. "Subsistence" means living off the land, and in rural indigenous communities it is both an economic necessity and a way to pass values and long-held food traditions from one generation to another. "Practiced for countless generations by the Native peoples of Alaska," writes the Alaska Federation of Natives, "(subsistence) continues to be the foundation of modern Alaska Native society and culture." The subsistence hunting project provided me with the means to travel to rural Alaska and gave me, through the generosity of the many people who opened their kitchens, the opportunity to study Alaska Native food.

The Alaska Natives, people of the Inupiat, Yup'ik, Siberian Yupik, Aleut, Athabascan, Alutiiq, Tlingit, Haida, and Tsimshian cultures, make up roughly 20 percent of the population of Alaska. The state has more biracial people, by percentage, than any other place besides Hawaii, according to the US Census. The majority of that group are Alaska Native and some other race. As racial identity grows more complex with each generation, the subsistence practices of gathering, processing, and sharing wild food becomes all the more important as a defining part of what it means to be Native.

After traveling and eating in rural Alaska, I began to notice the way Native subsistence values—self-reliance and interconnectedness with our neighbors and families, wild harvest, careful preparation for winter, attention to natural rhythms, sharing, and respect for the land and animals—repeatedly emerge within Alaska's wider food culture. Even more interesting, the most recent wave of immigrants settling in Alaska, many from parts of Asia and the Pacific Islands where fishing, sharing, gathering, and hunting are part of their tradition, bring value systems that echo existing subsistence ideals, with Alaska's urban fishery being a great example.

In 2017, I was given the opportunity to write for the *New York Times* Dining section. That led me to think about how Alaska's food culture is different from anywhere else. The more reporting I did, the more I saw how our isolated geography is a powerful influence on our food culture. We are experts at sourcing, substituting, and re-creating recipes.

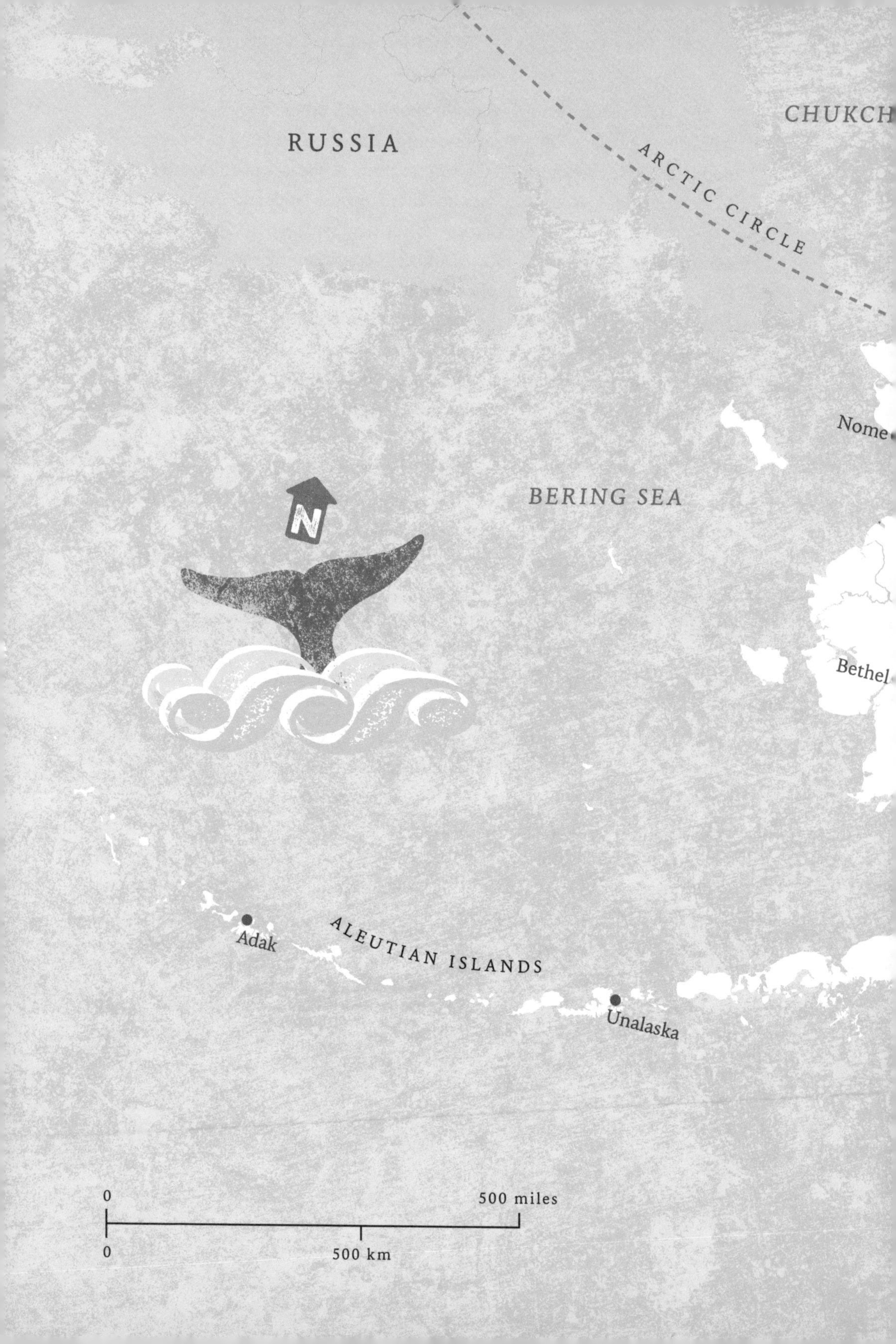

RUSSIA
CHUKCH
ARCTIC CIRCLE
Nome
BERING SEA
N
Bethel
Adak
ALEUTIAN ISLANDS
Unalaska
0
500 miles
0
500 km

Practicality and adaptation are strong currents in Alaska's foodways. Alaska's historic cookbooks, which provide inspiration for the recipes in this book, reflect an essential Alaska cooking dynamic, influenced paradoxically by the dependence on a limited produce and shelf-stable foods from Outside and an abundance of wild foods. The recipe writers are fond of using substitutions for hard-to-get ingredients, like cakes made with only a box mix and some lemon-lime soda because eggs are not easy to find. They also substitute wild ingredients into popular recipes, like sea lion meatballs or salmon-noodle casserole. This approach has provided us with a rich canon of uniquely Alaskan recipes.

When Krispy Kreme opened in Anchorage, my son was in kindergarten. We made a special trip, driving twenty minutes to the other side of town for our pilgrimage. A warm Krispy Kreme doughnut was a food I'd imagined a hundred times. It is a mundane experience for most Americans but a novelty in Alaska—a cultural reference point I didn't want him to miss out on.

When we got to the doughnut shop, there was a line out the door. We stood behind a couple of kids in doughnut costumes. Together we watched through the window the display of rising dough circles. Once they rose, the doughnuts rode down a conveyor belt into hot grease, took a flip, and then emerged into a shower of glaze. In a minute, they were in our hands, volcanically hot, sweet as love, light as air. My son took his first bite. I watched his face fill with pleasure. It was like nothing he'd ever tasted.

Chapter 1

In Alaska's Far-Flung Villages, Happiness Is a Cake Mix

In a modest boardinghouse on an Alaskan island just thirty miles across the sea from Russia, a handwritten order form hangs on the refrigerator. It has promotional photos of cakes a few women in the village have made that they can make for you: rectangles of yellow cake and devil's food cake enrobed in buttercream, with local nicknames piped out in pink: "Happy Birthday Bop-Bop" one reads. Another says "Happy Birthday Siti-Girl."

Traveling out here, where huge bones from bowhead whales litter the beach, I took a ninety-minute jet ride north from Anchorage and another hour by small plane over the Bering Sea. In this wild part of America, accessible only by water or air, there may not be plumbing or potable water, the local store may not carry perishables, and people may have to rely on caribou or salmon or bearded seal meat to stay fed. But no matter where you go in remote Alaska, you will always find a cake-mix cake.

Elsewhere, the American appetite for packaged baking mixes is waning, according to the market research firm Mintel, as consumers move away from packaged foods with artificial ingredients and buy more from in-store bakeries and specialty pastry shops. Yet in the small, mostly indigenous communities that dot rural Alaska, the box cake is a stalwart staple, the star of every community dessert table and a potent fund-raising tool.

At her home in Tanana, Cynthia Erickson and some young volunteers decorate a lemon-blueberry cake from a mix that she jazzes up.

"Cake mixes are the center of our little universe," said Cynthia Erickson, who owns the only grocery store in Tanana, an Athabascan village of three hundred on the Yukon River in central Alaska. "I have four damn shelves full."

In the wintertime, when Iditarod sled-dog mushers and Iron Dog snow machine racers pass through Tanana, everybody asks for Cynthia Erickson's rum cake. It's her mother's recipe, from the Athabascan village of Ruby, 120 miles downriver, made with yellow cake mix, vanilla instant pudding, and a half-cup of Bacardi.

Eating in rural Alaska is all about managing the expense and scarcity of store-bought food while trying to take advantage of seasonally abundant wild foods. Cash economies are weak, utilities and fuel are expensive, and many families live below the federal poverty line. To offset the cost of living, Alaska Natives here rely on traditional practices of hunting, fishing, and gathering. In a good year, they fill freezers with moose, berries, caribou, and salmon or marine mammals, depending on where they live. In a bad year, they have to buy more from the store.

The offerings in village stores often resemble those in the mini-marts or bodegas of America's urban food deserts, at two and three times the price. Food journeys in via jet, small plane, and barge. But milk and eggs spoil fast, and produce gets roughed up. Among the Hostess doughnuts, Spam, and soda, the cake mix is one of the few items on shelves everywhere that requires actual cooking. As a result, tricking out mixes has become a cottage industry, and many villages have a "cake lady" with her signature twist. Some bake as a hobby, while others do a brisk business selling cakes in places where getting to a bakery requires a plane ticket.

A sheet cake is decorated with berries to celebrate a teenager's birthday in the village of Gambell on St. Lawrence Island.

In the Far North, cake ladies top cakes with fondant photo prints of Inupiat whaling crews and serve them with mikigaq, barrel-fermented whale meat. On the western coast, mixes may be prepared with seagull eggs. In the Interior, pineapple upside-down cake is eaten with a salad made of lard, sugar, berries, and whitefish.

On a typical midsummer day in Tanana, people were hauling king salmon from their Yukon River fish wheels—a traditional wood device moored to the river shore that turns with the current and captures fish as they make their way upstream to spawn—then cutting and hanging up the salmon to smoke on the beach. Cynthia Erickson, who frequently bakes for Saint Aloysius Roman Catholic Church, was mopping up a load of thawing fresh produce that had come in frozen, a common shipping

Cynthia Erickson picks up supplies from the plane at the airport in Tanana. Eating in rural Alaska is all about managing the expense and scarcity of store-bought food while trying to take advantage of seasonally abundant wild foods.

hiccup for rural grocers. What to do with a load of icy bananas? Use them in a cake mix!

"Sometimes you don't have a lot of the stuff to make a regular cake," Cynthia Erickson said. "Maybe you don't have butter or you don't have milk." But with one substitution or another, you can always make a mix cake. Mayonnaise can take the place of an egg. Some recipes call for nothing but a mix and a bottle of Sprite. The Whole Foods crowd may judge it, she said, but where she lives it makes sense.

In Unalakleet, 300 miles west of Tanana on Norton Sound, Donna Erickson (no relation to Cynthia) is a noted cake lady. Her most famous creation was created in a rush to get to a community potluck. She made a white cake mix and poured it into a sheet pan because she knew it would bake quickly. After it was baked, she said, "I mixed orange Jell-O with two cups of bright orange salmonberries. I poured it on top of that cake and I threw it in the fridge. People were just like, 'Wow, can you make that again for me?'"

Fund-raisers known as cakewalks—a variation on musical chairs—are held to send whole basketball teams to the Lower 48, support people through chemotherapy, or pay for coffins. Rural Alaska has some of the highest rates of accidental death and suicide in the country. When there is tragedy in Unalakleet, bakers bring cakes to the school multipurpose room, put them on a big table, and each is given a number. Popular flavors include salmonberry, tundra blueberry, and low-bush cranberry.

Then the cakewalk begins: Each person buys a ticket, and then they all circle the table while music plays. When the music stops, a number is drawn out of an old coffee can. The person standing by the corresponding cake wins that one and the money goes to the fund-raising. Then the music starts again, and the cakewalk continues until all the cakes are gone. "It's a festive environment even though it's [sometimes] a sad time," said Donna Erickson. "You should see the cakes; they are so beautiful. Village bakers are brilliant."

In America's northernmost town, Utqiagvik (formerly called Barrow), the baker Mary Patkotak is brilliant at gaming cake economics. She uses Betty Crocker Triple Chocolate Fudge Cake Mix for her famous cherry-chocolate cake. In the village store, it costs four dollars and sixty-nine cents a box. On Amazon, where Ms. Patkotak orders it, it's one dollar and twenty-nine cents. Alaska's many weather delays mean the mix never shows up on time, but she doesn't care because the delay qualifies her for partial refunds on her annual Amazon Prime membership.

She bakes when she knows a payday is coming around, then freezes the cakes. Out-of-town customers order cakes or cupcakes from her Facebook page, and she retrieves them from the freezer and tucks them into the cargo hold of a small plane. "We don't have any bakeries. We have very few restaurants," she said. "People really crave the fresh cake."

Last winter, Cynthia Erickson hauled an old propane stove by snowmobile to her summer hunting camp, fifty miles northwest of Tanana on the Tozitna River. It fell apart on the way, but her husband wired it back together. She fired it up and slid in a chocolate cake.

It's a simple thing, making a cake from a box, she said, but when you're doing it in remote Alaska, you feel rich. "I was, like, the camp queen!" she said. "Middle of nowhere, eating cake."

MAKES 1 BUNDT CAKE

When I was growing up in the 1980s in Alaska, everybody's mother had a cake-mix cake recipe. Maybe it was the one that subs a 7-Up for all the ingredients, or the classic rum cake, where you put chopped nuts on the bottom and soak it with a glaze made of butter and Bacardi. Or the (giggle) Robert Redford cake, a.k.a. the "Better than Sex" cake, made with chocolate cake-mix cake soaked in condensed milk and topped with Cool Whip and candy bars. You can find these recipes in just about every Alaska community cookbook from mid-twentieth century on.

The one in my family line is simple: a never-fail poppy seed Bundt cake made famous in our immediate circles by my Aunt Alicia, who also grew up in Anchorage. Her recipe card lists yellow cake mix, butterscotch pudding mix, and extra eggs. Over the years, I've made it many, many times and it never tasted quite like hers. I came to believe it might have something to do with the fact that I can only find instant, artificially flavored butterscotch pudding mix in the store in Anchorage. So I set about looking for a substitute.

Cake-mix cakes are still relied on by Alaska cooks because, aside from the fact that they are very fast to put together, they call for easy-to-find, low-cost, mostly shelf-stable ingredients. Eggs are the only perishable thing (and, if you use a soda, you can get around that). You could make a pastry cream using brown sugar and it would be butterscotch pudding, but I wanted my re-tooled recipe to be true to the shelf-stable ingredient rule. That's how I settled on dulce de leche, a Mexican milk caramel. It comes in a small can and is widely available in the canned milk or Hispanic foods section of grocery stores. It tastes just right.

Some Bundt cake tips: Don't grease the pan with cooking spray. Use melted shortening or butter and

2 tablespoons melted butter or shortening, for the pan

2 tablespoons almond flour or all-purpose flour, for the pan

4 eggs

⅓ cup dulce de leche

1 cup water

½ cup canola oil

1 box yellow cake mix

⅓ cup poppy seeds

2 to 3 tablespoons powdered sugar, for dusting

brush it on with a pastry brush, then immediately flour the pan. (If you let the pan sit with the grease on it, it may pool in the bottom.) Almond flour, for flouring the pan, is nice because it is dark and so the baked Bundt cake looks perfect when you remove it from the pan. All-purpose flour tends to collect in white blobs on the surface of the baked cake. A general cake mix tip: Avoid using a standing mixer; it's almost impossible not to overbeat the mix. Instead, use a hand mixer or wooden spoon. Also, I've tried just about all the yellow box cake mixes out there, and it is my opinion that Betty Crocker Super Moist Yellow Cake Mix is by far the best for this recipe. Duncan Hines's yellow cake mix is a distant second. And, if you are making a gluten-free version of this cake, use King Arthur Yellow Cake Mix, which is great. Generally, canned dulce de leche is gluten free, but check the label.

Preheat the oven to 350°F. Brush the Bundt pan with melted butter, and then flour the pan with almond flour.

In a large bowl, beat the eggs and the dulce de leche until smooth, using a hand-held electric mixer or wooden spoon. Add the water, oil, cake mix, and poppy seeds, and mix until the batter is well combined and not lumpy. Don't overmix.

Pour the batter into the prepared pan. Bake for 38 to 40 minutes, until the cake springs back when pressed lightly on the top with your finger. Remove to a cooling rack for 5 minutes. Invert the cake on the rack, remove the pan, and let cool.

To serve, place the upside-down cake on a serving platter and dust with the powdered sugar.

Chapter 2

Whale Hunting at Point Hope, a Village Caught between Tradition and Climate Change

For the Inupiat villagers who for generations have made their homes on this finger of land in the Chukchi Sea, nothing is more important than the bowhead whale.

About nine hundred people live in Point Hope. The village store prices are double what people pay seven hundred miles south in Anchorage. A gallon of milk might be twelve dollars. Two pounds of hamburger patties, twenty-three dollars. In most homes, wild and foraged foods make up at least half the menu. The village has two stores, a school, several churches, and a restaurant that serves pizza, Chinese food, and hamburgers. Alcohol legally can't be possessed, sold, or imported.

Here the calendar revolves around seasons for hunting, fishing, and gathering. All year, the village looks forward to spring whaling, when crews of men thread through leads in the sea ice, quietly paddling in sealskin boats, looking for smooth black shapes rising out of the water.

The few massive bowhead whales taken by villagers each year supply thousands of pounds of dense protein. Beyond that, whale meat is considered an Alaska Native soul food. Hunting, butchering, and distributing the animal, village leaders say, is how elders teach young people the culture.

The blanket toss during the whaling feast in Point Hope

"Without the whale," said Steve Oomittuk, the former mayor of the village and former vice-president of the tribe, "we wouldn't be who we are."

In recent years, the much-anticipated whale hunt has run up against a warming Arctic. A bowhead can be sixty feet long and weigh seventy-five tons. Successful whaling crews have always hauled the massive animals onto the ice using a block and tackle, to butcher it. The last few seasons, the ice has been more unstable than elders in the village have ever seen. "It's getting harder and harder, the ice is thinner," Oomittuk said. "We can't pull up the whale."

Alaska had the hottest year on record in 2016, and every year since 2014 has had temperatures among the top ten warmest ever. In the Point Hope region, spring and summer temperatures have been on a warming trend since the 1980s. According to Rick Thoman, climate science and services manager for the National Weather Service in Alaska, what are now average

Slicing whale flipper on a sheet of plywood in Point Hope

summer temperatures would have been close to record-high temperatures in the mid-twentieth century.

The experience of hunters in Point Hope is part of a larger story being told by Alaska Natives in villages that rely on subsistence foods. Animal behavior is changing as the climate warms, and the windows of opportunity for certain types of hunting and fishing are shrinking. Lack of snow last winter grounded hunters for weeks because they couldn't travel by snowmobile. Changing ice conditions have complicated the walrus hunt so deeply, they've caused food shortages in some areas. Water has been creeping into ice cellars carved generations ago in what used to be permanently frozen ground, causing meat stored there to go bad. Meat and fish drying outside have been spoiled by rain.

"The twenty-four-hour daylight was a chance for us to hunt and gather all the different foods that migrate up north before the winter comes," Oomittuk said. "We see animals coming earlier; we see animals coming later; we see animals not coming at all. It has changed very fast."

Alaska Native cultures have adapted plenty over time and will continue to adapt, but climate change has become a formidable challenge to how people are used to getting their food in parts of Alaska, said Nicole Braem, who studies subsistence activities in the region for the State of Alaska. "It's about more than just meat . . . Traditional culture, language, all that stuff is at its strongest point with subsistence."

Point Hope took three whales in 2015, an acceptable harvest. In June at the annual feast to celebrate, elders sipped coffee and ate homemade doughnuts. Ron Oviok Sr., seventy-two, sat under a skin boat turned sideways to block the wind, going over the times he'd helped bring in a whale.

He says he can taste that whale meat kept in ice cellars is not staying as cold as it once did. Would grandchildren be able to continue the whale hunt as it had always been? Would great-grandchildren still have a taste for the meat?

"We try to keep the culture going as best we can," he said. "I'm glad hunters never give up."

Women make akutuq or "eskimo ice cream" with seal oil and caribou fat in Clark Lane's home.

Point Hope's people remain faithful to many long-held traditions. The town is still separated into two clans, each with its own whaling crews. Whaling feast activities happen at the same time every year, in two spots on either edge of town, each place designated for a different clan.

When a whaling captain is successful, he distributes meat to his family, the families of the whaling crews, and the community right after the hunt and during feast time. Whale is also shared communitywide at Thanksgiving, Christmas, and when the sea ice first forms—a date that seems to be later each year.

On the first day of the three-day June feast, four-wheelers buzzed villagers to the locations on the edges of town. On one side, Clark Lane, a whaling captain, and his crew members and family rose in front of a crowd to offer prayers of thanks. Women handed out pink-frosted cupcakes and dished mikigaq by the double-handful to people with outstretched ziplock bags. Mikigaq, or barrel-fermented whale meat, is a delicacy—inky black, shiny, and gelatinous in texture. Its taste is herbal, marine, and sour.

Bowhead whales have been the center of life in Point Hope for more than two thousand years. Before Christian missionaries came, bodies of dead Native whaling captains were laid out aboveground on whalebone scaffolds. Whalebones, along with lumber washed ashore from commercial whaling shipwrecks, braced the sod houses where many elders were born. Whale liver membrane is stretched across drums that are used for songs and dances. Curved bowhead jawbones, tall as trees, now mark the graves of whaling captains and encircle the village cemetery. The school mascots are the Harpooners and the Harpoonerettes.

During feast time, women related to a whaling captain's crew work nearly around the clock preparing whale and other traditional foods to share. On the first evening, Clark Lane's home was crowded with women at work. As an episode of *Barefoot Contessa* played on the big-screen TV, they pulled big metal bowls of melted caribou fat from the oven and set them on the floor. As soon as the liquid fat cooled enough to be touched, they began to whip air into it with their hands, making akutuq—Eskimo ice cream. When the fat took on the texture of whipped butter, they drizzled in seal

FOLLOWING: Young villagers check their cellphones.

Whaling captain Isaac Killigvuk in front of his canoe

oil, added meat or berries, and then chilled it. It would be sliced and served on the second day, while men cut and distributed whale flipper.

Jana Koenig, Clark Lane's daughter, a mother of six in her thirties, has been making akutuq for the last few years, having been trained by her aunt. "Young people don't respect traditions around whaling as they once did," she said.

It used to be, for example, that the village listened for the sound of the church bell during hunting time, a signal that everyone should go down to the beach to help bring in the meat. Now, some crew members post on Facebook before the bell.

"I don't agree with that," she said.

Her husband is an emergency responder in the village and his job pays decently, she said. Still, they rely on gull eggs, seal oil, berries, caribou, and whale, among other foods, to feed their family.

Clark Lane is also the vice-president of the Point Hope village corporation, called Tikigaq. He began helping a whaling crew as a boy. In those days, the crew would spend weeks out on the ice. His first job was as a "boyer," an errand boy, tasked with small jobs like keeping the fire going and getting seal oil for the lamp. He worked his way up to the boat over time. He never wanted to become a captain, but four years ago his mother chose him to do it. "This crew is yours; you're taking it over no matter what," she told him.

Now he leads a crew of twenty-seven. During the whaling season, which usually begins in April and lasts until June, ten of them will hunt at a time, paddling a skin boat. When they see a whale surfacing to breathe, they will chase it if they are close enough. Otherwise they will follow it, careful not to give themselves away by hitting the boat with their paddles.

Harpooning requires practice. They must be within ten feet of the animal to shoot it from the harpoon gun. When the harpoon strikes the whale, a core filled with explosive powder detonates, usually killing the animal instantly. After that, the crew will haul the carcass onto the ice and slice the meat into pieces that can be taken to shore. "It takes about a day and a half to get it all sorted out," Clark Lane said.

Meat is then distributed, and some is stored in ice cellars for community gatherings. Lane is responsible for keeping his crew fed during the hunt. If he didn't have subsistence foods to share with them during that time, it would be too expensive to hunt. "Sure I go to the store and buy processed food, but I love my Inupiat food. I love the whale, beluga. I love the caribou. I love the walrus. I love the birds, all the birds. I love to pick their eggs," he said.

He, too, has noticed big changes in the seasons and the ice, but he sees it as part of a long natural cycle. He says he's seen warm winters and short seasons before. "I don't believe in climate change," he said. "I really don't."

A more realistic worry for whaling would be an oil spill from an offshore arctic drilling rig, he said. Shell Oil drilling in the Chukchi Sea. (At the time, such drilling had been conditionally approved by the Obama administration, and Shell was exploring it. The company pulled out late that year, citing costs and other difficulties.)

Clark Lane wasn't against drilling, he said. It was progress. Inevitable. Just like motorized boats, cable TV, cell phones, indoor plumbing. He just hoped it would be done responsibly. "I don't want to live the way I did long time ago. I had no running water. I had to haul it every day," he said. "A lot

Eva Kevovach gathers beluga whale meat to give to elders.

of people say they could turn back; I don't think so. I could make it, but not a lot of people, not my kids."

The third day of the feast was for giving thanks and games. Men drank coffee, ate, and talked. Women worked in a large outdoor kitchen, cutting meat from bearded seal, whale, and birds with sharp, round ulu blades. Whale meat and entrails boiled over open fires. In the afternoon, children lined up for races across the grass.

Clark's son, Jacob Lane, twenty-two, watched the children run. He went out in the whaling boat for the first time as a senior in high school. Before that, he thought whaling was boring and preferred playing Call of Duty on his Xbox. He remembered the exact moment he changed his mind on that first run. "We were breaking thin sheets of ice while paddling," he said. "It was really hard, but it was really fun. You get sore. Damn sore."

The biggest threat to the whaling tradition Jacob Lane sees is the distraction caused by technology like video games and the Internet. But it is the same technology that allowed him to see how Inupiat whaling culture has been misunderstood by the outside world. It isn't like commercial whaling or sport hunting, he said. "We're feeding a whole village."

Anna Sattler
ALASKA NATIVE HOME COOK

Anna Sattler, who is Yup'ik by heritage, grew up in remote Southwestern Alaska, in the villages of Tuntutuliak, Platinum, Bethel, and Kwethluk, and now lives in Anchorage. She hosts *Anna's Alaska: Off the Eaten Path*, an Alaska Native cooking show series on Facebook and YouTube. Her videos illustrate a number of things that make Alaska home cooking unique. She frequently tells the story of gathering, hunting, processing, and preserving wild foods as part of the cooking process for a recipe. Those things are an outsized part of kitchen culture here. And, she often re-envisions classic recipes—like stroganoff, spaghetti sauce, and baked French toast—to include both commonly available shelf-stable ingredients, like canned milk, as well as wild foods, like caribou, moose, and salmonberries. That kind of recipe adaptation is a hallmark of Alaska cooking.

Julia: When you think back to growing up in your village, when did you first begin to understand the process of preserving foods, and is there a particular food that comes to mind?

Anna: Fish, salmon. I learned how to process fish traditionally by being with my relatives and watching them carry out their whole process of preserving it. My favorite food is half-smoked salmon. I take a salmon and cut it into strips. And I hang it up and let it air dry. Then I brine it, and the brine I use is rock salt in water, which is so thick a potato will float in it. I put the air-dried salmon strips in the brine overnight, and then I let them air dry again for two to three days until they're past tacky. Then I put the salmon in the smokehouse for two or three days, until it's almost fully cured. It's not like lox, and it's not kippered—it's in between. Then I cut the strips up, and can them or freeze them.

Julia: Can you take yourself back to when you first remember that taste in your mouth? When do you remember having half-smoked salmon as a taste you understood?

Anna: You know, I think it was when my dad moved me to Colorado for the first semester of kindergarten to learn English. And being in Colorado and being away from salmon and moose, the only way I would eat any kind of beef was if my grandparents or aunts and uncles told me it was moose meat. That's when I realized that salmon and moose are intrinsically ingrained in my whole body. I have to have those foods. They are part of me and make me feel good.

Julia: So take me through the process of getting a moose. How does that work?

Anna: My dad did it the scary way. He would call them in and rub branches together. And so they would charge us. I like to hunt when the moose is nice and calm, because then they're not tense and the meat is much better. So you shoot whatever legal moose is out there and then you gut it, cut it up, quarter it, get it back home, and then process it. I always process it myself, moose for burger all the way up to T-bones. To this day I still have to take a picture or video of what I am cutting and send it to my dad or someone else, and say, "This is the brisket, right?"

Julia: How long does it take to process a moose?

Anna: It depends on how many people are there. If it's just me and maybe an occasional friend, it'll take a good week. I just sawed up some soup bones with the Sawzall, just the arm and the leg of a moose, and it took me two nights.

Julia: Let's say you are going to describe Alaska's cuisine. How do Alaskans eat, from your point of view?

Anna: We eat largely from the land. The spring, summer, and fall is the time when we get all of our foods and prepare them for the entire winter, from ptarmigan to beach greens, berries, all the fish, game, all of that stuff. That's my definition of Alaskan eating. And then everything homegrown, you know, from the valley. I love going to those [farmers'] markets and getting all the foods that I'm not getting myself.

Julia: Talk to me about your memories of shelf-stable foods you had when you were a kid—things we all have a soft spot for, like Spam or canned fruit cocktail or pilot bread.

Anna: Yes, my favorite still to this day is canned evaporated milk. I love canned fruit and vegetables, because when we were growing up by the time apples and oranges got to the store, they were shriveled up little things. A can of fruit was—you know, I love it—but I think probably the number one is canned milk. I have tons here. I substitute it for anything cream-based— like overnight salmonberry French toast. And I would use canned milk for ptarmigan enchiladas. I would prepare everything and then just pour a can of evaporated milk over it. In my coffee, everything. I don't even use a bottle of milk. I use canned milk.

Julia: Can you talk about what, in your mind, are subsistence values and the ways you see them reflected in Alaska's wider relationship with food?

Anna: Why are rural Alaskans so reliant on subsistence? Not only because it's part of our culture but because of the cost of food. You know, in rural

Alaska a gallon of milk in a large community like Bethel costs eleven dollars and a gallon of gasoline is six dollars. Food is more expensive than heating your home or fueling your vehicle. Subsistence is a necessity when a loaf of bread costs, you know, seven dollars, compared with being able to make it yourself. Or berries, a small bag of berries, frozen berries, costs twenty-two dollars, but you can go out and pick hundreds of gallons of free berries. I mean that it's a necessity in rural Alaska. Beyond that, I don't know if the right word is spirituality or just, you know, part of who you are. It's ingrained in my whole being, to be able to get these kinds of foods from the land and prepare them in ways I'm able to share with my elders and the people I love.

SALMON POT PIE WITH PARMESAN CRUST

SERVES 6 TO 8

Looking through Alaska's old cookbooks, especially those from Southeast Alaska, Homer, Kodiak, and the Aleutians, I've found many recipes for a Russian-influenced salmon pie, often called peroke or pirok. Researching it further, I think it's one of a handful of dishes that has taken on a life of its own in Alaska, becoming more regional over time.

Many recipes use puff pastry and many include a sliced boiled egg. Most can accommodate canned or raw salmon. Smoked salmon works too. All of them rely on vegetables that grow well in Alaska, including cabbage, onions, celery, carrots, and potatoes. I was able to find all my ingredients at the farmers' market.

My version of salmon pie, which uses a Parmesan crust, isn't all that traditional; it's more pirok-inspired than actual pirok. The recipe is easy to modify. You can use store-bought crust or puff pastry if you're in a hurry. Add a layer of Yukon Gold potatoes sliced on a mandoline if you like. Or a layer of thinly sliced carrots. Some people don't feel right if there are no green peas in it. You can also use brown or wild rice. My family isn't really into the boiled egg, so I skip it, but you could layer one on.

This dish is kind of a showstopper and a great way to stretch salmon

CRUST:

Roughly 4 ounces grated (about a ½ cup)
   Parmesan cheese
1 stick (½ cup) cold butter, chopped
1½ cups flour
2 teaspoons dried thyme
¼ to ½ cup cold water
One egg, beaten, for brushing on top crust

FILLING:

1 tablespoon bacon fat, or two slices
   bacon, diced
2 cups chopped cabbage
½ large white onion (about 1 cup), diced
1 small leek, white part only, well rinsed
   and diced
1 rib celery, finely chopped
2 cups chopped fresh mushrooms
Salt
Pepper
1 tablespoon butter
1 tablespoon flour
1¼ cups seafood stock, or vegetable stock
   or chicken stock
1 teaspoon dried thyme
1 cup cooked rice (white, brown, or wild)
10 to 12 ounces raw salmon, chopped, or
   canned, or smoked (if you use smoked,
   don't add salt to the vegetables)
½ cup cream

to feed a crowd. (It's also a good use for canned salmon or spring freezer salmon.) Oh, and the secret to great flavor: bacon fat. That comes straight from a 100-year-old cookbook. If you don't have any on hand, try a couple slices of bacon.

FOR THE CRUST: At least 3 hours before you plan to eat, in the bowl of a food processor (or blender), grind the Parmesan cheese until it's fine. Add the butter, flour, and thyme, and pulse into a fine meal. Drizzle the water into the mixture (with the blade spinning) until it forms a ball. (I don't recommend making this crust by hand.)

Divide the crust into two rounds, wrap in plastic wrap, and chill in the refrigerator for at least 1 hour. (If you're in a pinch, the freezer for 20 minutes works, too.)

FOR THE FILLING: About an hour and a half before dinner, preheat the oven to 350°F.

Over medium heat in a large skillet, melt the bacon fat. Add the cabbage, onion, leek, celery, and mushrooms, and sauté until soft, about 10 minutes. Season generously with salt and pepper.

Meanwhile, in a small saucepan over medium heat, melt the butter and whisk in the flour to form a paste. Pour in the stock, add the thyme, and whisk to combine. Allow to boil and thicken, stirring frequently, and remove from the heat.

Remove the dough rounds from the refrigerator. On a floured work surface, roll out one of the dough rounds and line a 9-inch pie pan. In the bottom crust, layer the rice, salmon, and vegetables. Pour the stock mixture over, and drizzle the cream over the top. Roll out the second dough round and cover the pie. Crimp the top and bottom edges together to seal. Cut some small steam vents in the top crust. Brush the top crust with the beaten egg.

Bake for 40 minutes. Remove to a cooling rack. Cool for at least 10 minutes before serving.

Chapter 3

Finding Produce in Alaska's Winters Takes Wiles and Luck

In February, when the sun doesn't edge over the mountains until midmorning and starts to sink only a few hours later, Anchorage feels a little like one big, icy strip-mall parking lot with a tremendous mountain view. It's so cold that the steering wheel hurts to touch. Life plays out under streetlight instead of daylight, and the rest of the world seems twice as far away as it did when the leaves were green.

Talk to anybody and the conversation veers into two intertwined ideas: vacation and food. Alaskans are lusting after fresh fruits and vegetables right now, fantasizing about the pepper and snap of an arugula stem and the sweet acid of a juicy mango. They crave simple things that shoppers in the Lower 48—where grocery stores are restocked daily with produce brought in from greenhouses and farms—can get their hands on with just a short drive or a swipe on an app. Even in this cosmopolitan city of 350,000, people who like to cook spend the moonlit mornings before work scrolling through Instagram pictures of faraway blood oranges and heirloom tomatoes.

For Carlyle Watt, the executive chef and head baker at Fire Island Rustic Bakeshop, it's a ripe pear. "It would be a D'Anjou or a Bosc, something

FOLLOWING: The produce section at a Fred Meyer store in Anchorage. Grocers have to troubleshoot constantly to prevent "out of stocks."

Carlyle Watt, executive chef and head baker at Fire Island Rustic Bakeshop in Anchorage. His approach to winter cooking is to embrace the austerity and master what's left in the root cellar and freezer.

run-of-the-mill," he said on a recent afternoon as snowflakes feathered down outside the bakery window. "I would touch it and it would just kind of yield to my thumb, and then I would take a bite of it right there in the store and I would have to make a little slurping sound, so not all the juice would run down my chin, but some would."

A feeling of deprivation is part of the psychological cycle of life in Alaska. In summertime, farmers' market tables overflow with greens, and garden zucchini swell to the size of small dogs in the all-night light. But late winter is the season of austerity and anticipation. Though each day brings a few more minutes of light, the root-cellar stock has dwindled to last summer's dry-skinned beets, gnarled carrots, and potatoes with eyes. All those blocks of frozen sockeye in the chest freezer don't have the same appeal they did in November.

The grocery store isn't a perfect solution. Though communities in rural Alaska rely heavily on wild foods, the majority of the population, living in

Kim Sunée, left, a cookbook author, has text relationships with supermarket produce workers who let her know when certain fresh items arrive. Here she shops at a Safeway with one of her produce contacts, Danny Noblett.

cities and towns, relies on food from outside the state. According to the Alaska Food Policy Council, about 95 percent of all the food Alaskans eat comes from somewhere else. The bulk of it travels by highway to Seattle, then floats roughly 1,600 miles north by sea, a trip that can take a week inside a dark container. By the time it gets here, tomatoes have become ghosts, their flesh pinkish and watery. Avocados are hard but rotten around the pit. Boxed, prewashed lettuces arrive often with an odor of decay.

Despite these bumps and bruises, fresh food is expensive, and there isn't always enough—especially on Sunday afternoons, when whole swaths of the produce section are frequently bare.

Kate Consenstein, who owns a communications business in Anchorage, believes in eating seasonally, but then something comes over her when she glimpses an exotic fruit among the waxy apples and leathery oranges in Safeway, like a four-leaf clover in the grass. "When you live in Alaska and, like, a dragon fruit waves at you from a stack at the grocery store, I run at it," she said. "I'm moved by its gravitational pull. I want that sweet brightness. I want it in my mouth. Then I get to the register and it's twenty freaking dollars. And I am like, so be it."

Fruit and vegetables come to one of Alaska's largest grocers, Fred Meyer, in just two or three weekly shipments, said Steve Lacy, the food safety manager. The challenge of keeping food fresh and costs down, and dealing with unexpected delays caused by weather or shipping breakdowns, forces grocers to troubleshoot constantly, he said. Between shipments, stores can't always keep up with demand. "Out of stock," the grocery business term for empty shelves, is a fact of life. The farther from Anchorage shoppers are, the more often they encounter them. "There's just no way around it," Steve Lacy said.

Leah Glasscock-Sanders, a recess attendant at a charter school in Wasilla, an Anchorage suburb, always plans her shopping in the early mornings to get the best selection. Even so, she sometimes can't find what she needs. "It's cleaned out," she said. "There might be five bell peppers to choose from when I get there, and they would all be of a quality I wouldn't purchase."

Resourceful Alaskans find a way to get the produce they've been fantasizing about. Pineapples peek out of carry-on luggage. Meyer lemons arrive from relatives by FedEx. An Alaskan might forgo a latte to pay five dollars for a single perfect Sumo mandarin orange, flown in by New Sagaya, the city's largest gourmet market.

Deprivation also leads to unusual relationships. Maybe there's a "peach guy" you meet in a parking lot, and you trade seventy dollars in cash for a case of what's in his trunk. Or, if you live way up north, you may plead on Facebook for someone, anyone, to tuck an avocado into a pocket when he gets on a bush plane to your village. And you may think about it for days until it arrives, as you watch Giada and the *Barefoot Contessa* on cable. And then, after you thank whoever brought you the avocado with some caribou meat from your freezer, you may cut it in half and share it with your best friend, keeping it a secret from the children.

About three years ago Kim Sunée, a memoirist and cookbook author, entered into an inventory-related texting relationship with some supermar-

The spicy chorizo and red lentil soup from Maya Wilson's *The Alaska from Scratch Cookbook* features carrots, a root cellar staple, which grow unusually sweet in Alaska's climate.

ket produce workers. Soon she was bringing the green-aproned men a quiche or a pan of lemon-raspberry rolls with cream cheese frosting. Now a little buzz in her pocket tells her when the store has a clutch of fresh organic figs, or white asparagus or pea shoots or passion fruit. "You have to cultivate these relationships when you are living in a place like this," she said.

Kim Sunée still spends good money on mail order from the New York deli Russ & Daughters. Once, she carried a leg of Prosciutto di Parma all the way from Italy. "Let's just say I've smuggled back some things," she said.

Maya Wilson moved to Nikiski, south of Anchorage, from California in 2011 to help pastor a church. The grocery store was more than an hour away, and so she started a blog, *Alaska from Scratch*, tapping into her feelings of isolation, and making recipes for things she craved but couldn't easily find, like pumpkin spice coffee creamer and pillowy Lofthouse sugar cookies.

Allison Warden pulling a frozen king salmon from her freezer. She wrapped the fish with a handle so she could bring it as carry-on on a flight from Dillingham.

Her blog audience grew every day, and her Instagram feed now has more than 54,000 followers. Isolation stokes her imagination, she said; cravings motivate her. They make Alaska a perfect laboratory for writing recipes. No pine nuts? Use pistachios. No lemons? Try oranges. "I cannot tell you how many times I envisioned a recipe and I went to the store and I couldn't find the ingredients," Ms. Wilson said. "I was so spoiled in California. Alaska has made me a much more self-sufficient human being."

It used to be worse. Maybe fifty years ago, most winter vegetables and fruit came frozen or in a can. Many Anchorage children first encountered cherries, for example, in canned fruit cocktail, waxy and pink.

Allison Warden, an artist and rapper who lives in Anchorage, is Inupiaq, with roots in the Far North village of Kaktovik. She lives with her mother, and they share a freezer full of wild foods: caribou, walrus, seal, whitefish, duck, seal liver, and whale, mostly supplied by family. When money is tight in winter, Ms. Warden finds herself eating traditional proteins and rice, but her fantasies are full of tropical fruit. She still remembers eating her first mango, when she was twenty-eight, on a trip to New York. "It was the most amazing thing ever that I never thought I could ever taste," she said.

Carlyle Watt, the chef at Fire Island bakery, is originally from South Carolina. He decided years ago to lean into Alaska's extremes rather than resist them. His approach to winter cooking is to embrace the austerity and master what's left in the root cellar and freezer. "You learn what potato to get in order to get that perfect crispy exterior and the buttery interior," he said. "You figure out that roasting a whole carrot until it turns black is delicious."

Alaska summers, short and lush, are electric, the long days packed with activity. In winter, Mr. Watt said, you get to catch your breath and revel in the slowness. You study the incremental return of the light, enjoy anticipation, get drunk on spring when it comes. Once you understand how all that works, you can call yourself Alaskan.

"This is your penance," he said. "You get through it. Then you're rewarded, slowly at first with a few radishes and maybe a little bit of greens, and later with, like . . . everything. You are paying your dues to be a local in the summertime."

Bob Ripley
SUPPLIER OF ALASKA'S PANTRIES AND PRODUCE FANTASIES

Bob Ripley is the general manager of Costco Wholesale on Dimond Boulevard in Anchorage. He's worked at Costco for thirty years, mostly in Alaska. He started out bringing carts in from the parking lot in 1989. Ripley is deeply familiar with the distinct Alaska practice of pantry stocking. Alaskans, especially those in rural places, keep deep pantries as a matter of custom, supplied with shelf-stable foods. They spend more on bulk food purchases than residents of other states. Ripley has a window onto how Alaska's isolation and the complications of keeping fresh grocery store shelves stocked cause Alaskans to long for certain foods, fresh produce in particular. He also has a deep familiarity with Alaska Costco shoppers' special yearning for hunting, fishing, and food-processing equipment and a fanatical allegiance to local Alaska seafood—both signs of the way Alaska's food culture is especially connected to the wild world.

Julia: As you watch all these people shop at Costco, what do you think about how Alaskans regard food?

Bob: I think it's unique in Alaska, and I didn't really realize that until I spent some time in a Michigan Costco where shopping habits are a little different. You know, Alaskans are unique in the way they buy shelf-stable and frozen foods that are going to last. The folks here come from a long distance away and have to get their supplies home and have them last for a while.

Julia: Can you talk more about Alaskans' psychology in relation to food and pantry stocking, and how bulk shopping fits in?

Bob: I would like to think that Alaskans are more buyer-aware than in other places I've been. They've got to think long-term. They have to think of extremes, you know? I've been to a lot of rural Alaska and I've seen a

lot of freezers and places to store food. When I was living Outside, I didn't really see that there. Here there's a lot of thinking about those things before they travel and shop. They tend to buy more of particular items from our candy section where we have our cookies and crackers. There's a particular approach Alaskans use to buying items specifically off our sales floor versus fresh-baked in our bakery because those items are just not shelf-stable.

Julia: Can you talk about people buying bulk rice? Like what kind of eaters buy that rice?

Bob: It's pretty remarkable the amount of rice that is sold here. I don't know if you remember about ten years ago, there was a big rice shortage. They could not send me enough rice. Even though there wasn't a shortage, it became a shortage because of panic buying. A lot of it was just regular folks who needed to fill their pantry and thought, how am I going to get through the next three months if I don't have that fifty-pound bag of rice? Alaskan shoppers are very savvy and they understand value. That fifty-pound bag of rice, if you price that out at a local grocery store, it's sometimes three, four, five times the cost.

Julia: Are there other ways that certain shopping habits pronounced in rural Alaska have an influence on urban buyers?

Bob: I would say mostly the shelf-stable items. In most of America, you know, Tang or Kool-Aid isn't the drink of choice. But those are some of our top sellers, those powder drinks. It's really amazing.

Julia: Are there certain foods that you carry here that you know are particularly Alaskan?

Bob: Well, one item for rural Alaska is pilot bread. It's not sold in any of our other Northwest Costco locations. It's only carried in Anchorage now, but it'll be in Fairbanks when they open up in a couple weeks. And it's pretty amazing how sensitive [an issue] canned fish can be, besides tuna fish. We carried canned salmon in the past. We were accidentally shipped some canned salmon that was not wild Alaskan salmon; it was farmed, and there was an uproar, rightfully so.

Julia: So another thing that has come up a lot, regarding how Alaska looks at food, is this thread of people really desiring foods that are hard to get here. Have you had experience with certain foods that have come into Costco that people just freaked out about?

Bob: It's so hard to find produce. Especially we're just talking about Fairbanks. You know, I was up there and every time I would go into Fred Meyer or Walmart, the shelves were bare. It's hard for them to judge what's needed. People really appreciate fresh oranges and fresh bananas and things like that, but then when you start bringing in the other items that people can try, it's like, man, I can get squash in Alaska in November for Thanksgiving? That's awesome. For a lot of years, we weren't able to offer that.

Julia: If you were going to describe Alaska's food culture, what would you say?

Bob: I think Alaskans are good at the basics. You look at a pantry and it has all the things that you should have in it. But then you find some unique items in the freezer. You know, you're not going to see somebody with a ten-pound case of king crab in their freezer in Utah. We're the largest seller of king crab of any Costco market by a wide margin.

Julia: So there's a wild food component to how people eat here in Alaska that might be different from other places related to food culture?

Bob: I would say in general, it's similar to other places, but in Alaska, customers buy wild foods in more bulk. They buy more of it. We put a dollar amount to every basket that passes through, you know, and Alaska is far and away the leader in the number of items per basket. It's higher than you see anywhere else. I don't know if that's just because people are traveling from a distance to get their things and they're not going to come as often. But I think that our Alaskan shopping habits kind of lean that way.

THE ALASKA COCKTAIL

MAKES 1 MARTINI

Recently, I have become obsessed with the delicious pre-Prohibition version of a martini called the Alaska Cocktail, which led me to some serious gin research. I discovered that, like Baked Alaska, the drink is not representative of our state's cuisine. It was, instead, named for what our state represented in the cultural imagination at that time. (Baked Alaska, developed by a chef in New York City, was meant to commemorate the 1867 purchase of the state.) The Alaska Cocktail is a creative take on a martini: stiff, complex, cold, and golden as a prospector's dreams.

The recipe first appeared in a 1913 book by bartender Jacques Straub called *Straub's Manual of Mixed Drinks*. You can also find it in *The Savoy Cocktail Book*, a classic encyclopedia of cocktail recipes, originally published in the 1930s. It's made with three ingredients: Old Tom Gin (a sweeter, less juniper-forward gin), yellow Chartreuse, and orange bitters. *Savoy* says, "So far as can be ascertained this delectable potion is NOT the staple diet of the Esquimaux [check THAT spelling!]."

Chartreuse has its own mysterious cocktail story. The short version is that the recipe for this liqueur involved 130 herbs, soaked in alcohol, and only two monks sworn to secrecy know what they are.

With the help of a group of friends in the backyard, I developed two recipes, one more traditional and drier, and one less traditional, sweeter, more golden, and herbal (my personal favorite). I made the two versions of this cocktail with two of Alaska's very good local gins: one lovely sweet gin from Amalga Distillery in Juneau made with devil's club, Labrador tea, and iris

CHAPTER 3 ⚬ 48

root, and another delicious gin, 50 Fathoms, from Port Chilkoot Distillery in Haines made with juniper, coriander, cinnamon, and spruce tips. Both of them are fantastic! I use a jigger to measure the liquid ingredients, but you have to estimate a little to get a ¼ ounce.

ALASKA COCKTAIL (TRADITIONAL VERSION)

2¼ ounces 50 Fathoms Gin
¾ ounce yellow Chartreuse
1 dash Angostura Orange Bitters
Lemon twist

Add a handful of ice cubes to a shaker. Pour the gin, Chartreuse, and bitters over the ice, cover, and shake briefly to chill.

Strain into a chilled martini glass. Serve with the lemon twist.

ALASKA COCKTAIL (O'MALLEY VERSION)

2 ounces Amalga Distillery Gin
1 ounce yellow Chartreuse
2 dashes Angostura Orange Bitters
Lemon twist

Mix and serve as for the traditional Alaska Cocktail.

Chapter 4

Alaska Sprouts: The Future of Food Sprouts in Deep Winter

Snow may still be melting in Anchorage, but in SJ Klein's world right now, delicate green shoots spiral out of seeds, split into tender leaves, and reach toward the pull of white light. This springtime process plays out every few weeks, year-round, in the controlled environment of Klein's hydroponic microgreen farm. He has been operating an urban sprout farm for eight years, and his business, Alaska Sprouts, now supplies most of the restaurants in Anchorage. Klein's greens turn up in sushi rolls, sub sandwiches, bowls of pho, and atop seafood specials at high-end bistros. "I guess we feed Anchorage. It's not a deep niche, but it's a big enough niche so we can do it," he said.

The soilless indoor growing process of hydroponics relies on nutrient-rich water and artificial light. It is resource intensive, in particular because of the cost of electricity. It takes certain market conditions to make an operation pencil out, Klein said. In Anchorage, for example, a combination of the distance from outside producers, loyal local food enthusiasts, and a growing Asian demographic makes it possible.

In early February, a full moon rises over the Arctic community of Kotzebue and beyond it a frozen Kotzebue Sound and beyond that the Chukchi Sea.

According to Klein, Alaska Sprouts has an edge over outside producers because of quality. Sprouts are delicate and shipping can damage or freeze them. He's worked hard to develop a reputation for having a product that is reliably fresh and available. "If you can supply people with what they need consistently, you're going to grow," Klein said. "Alaska Sprouts grows 10 to 15 percent each year," he added.

Klein's acreage consists of stacks of carefully tended, illuminated trays, and large barrels for sprouting mung beans and clover, which require darkness. The biggest crop he grows is mung beans. The next largest is clover sandwich sprouts. He also grows daikon, onion, a sprouted three-bean mix, and a microgreen salad mix made of tiny kale, bok choy, and wasabi plants. Outside of restaurants, his products are at farmers' markets and on the shelves at numerous Asian groceries, Carrs-Safeway locations, Red Apple Market, and New Sagaya.

Sprout farming isn't easy. Seeds are an agricultural product and can carry bacteria. Klein, who says he's been a chemistry nerd since childhood, tests his sprouts for bacterial pathogens in a small lab every day. His growing facility must be kept obsessively clean. "The whole goal is that people see our sprouts in the store and know that it's safe," Klein declared.

One of the attractions of sprouts for consumers is their concentrated nutritional value, he continued. Broccoli sprouts, for example, have 250 times the antioxidants of mature broccoli. "Pound for pound, sprouts just have more of it," he said. And, as the produce selection thins in grocery stores in wintertime, anything fresh has appeal.

Klein, forty-six, didn't plan to be a sprout farmer. He grew up in Anchorage and attended Harvard, studying political economics and international relations. He also went to school for brewing beer and, for a while, ran the Borealis Brewery. The beer venture failed but taught him about business. While selling beer, he struck up a friendship with Bernie Souphanavong, owner of Bernie's Bar in downtown Anchorage. Souphanavong had been growing sprouts for years and was well connected in the city's Asian communities. He saw a growing market for sprouts there. "He knew there was a need thirty years ago," Klein said. "The population for whom this food is a staple has grown."

Klein's business has also benefited from a demographic shift over the past thirty years, which powered a boom in Asian restaurants and groceries.

Sprouts and herbs grow in Alaska Sprouts' Anchorage warehouse.

One in ten people in Anchorage is Asian. The largest slice of this group has Filipino roots, followed by Koreans and Southeast Asians from Thailand, Laos, and Vietnam. This demographic shift powered a boom in Asian restaurants and grocery stores and influenced the eating and cooking habits of the overall population, Klein explained. "We're in more places, more people are eating sprouts, and this pho thing has just taken off," he added.

The key is experimenting while also paying careful attention to what consumers want. Some of Klein's favorite products, like raw soy milk and pumpkin sprouts, were delicious but couldn't gain a foothold in the market. "The joy of entrepreneurship is doing something new and different and

FOLLOWING: Klein calls his operation, tucked inside a warehouse along a busy artery in Anchorage, an urban sprout farm.

SJ Klein, urban sprout farmer and owner of Alaska Sprouts. Klein's sprouts are found on grocery store shelves and in the majority of restaurants in Anchorage.

helping people discover it," he said. "The skills it takes to do entrepreneurship to bring something new into the world are totally different from the skills needed to keep a business going."

Klein has been happy to see successful hydroponic growers in rural Alaska communities like Kotzebue and St. Paul. Rural Alaska is ripe for hydroponics for some of the same reasons that Klein's business has been successful in Anchorage. "When you get that far out on the margins, the cost to produce isn't too much more than the cost to ship it up, and the quality is much better," Klein explained.

For years Klein operated his business out of a dog-eared warehouse in Spenard. But this spring, betting on the growing appreciation of local foods that has buoyed his business, he opened a new retail/manufacturing facility in a space shared with the ice cream company Wild Scoops and Alaska Pasta Company in Anchorage's Fairview neighborhood. One of the challenges for small local food operations is the lack of space, he said. The shared location will be the city's first local food retail/manufacturing location of its kind.

"The farmers' markets have probably driven it more than anything else," Klein said. "Farmers' markets have really given people an opportunity to experiment, both with people making stuff and people trying new things."

Elissa Brown, owner of Wild Scoops, first met Klein when she approached him to buy his hydroponic basil for her ice cream. "I think a lot of the successful food companies rely on a network of other food set-ups," she said. "It makes sense there would be a storefront like this where we are all right next to each other."

Klein, she said, is a pioneer in local food production with a tested business model. "He found a way to produce a fresh product year-round in Anchorage," Brown marveled. "That's impressive."

Aaron Apling-Gilman
EXECUTIVE CHEF DEFINING "ALASKA CUISINE" IN A RESTAURANT KITCHEN

Aaron Apling-Gilman is executive chef at Seven Glaciers restaurant, a fine dining institution a tram ride up Mount Alyeska in Girdwood, Alaska. He is an avid fisherman and hunter, skills he learned from his grandparents, and he also often forages for local edibles, including mushrooms, fiddleheads, and berries. Like many chefs in Alaska's small cohort of fine dining restaurants, he relies on as many local purveyors and farmers as possible, incorporating ingredients sourced from Kenai to the Matanuska-Susitna Valley. His goal at his restaurant is to create dishes that help bring definition to Alaska's unique cuisine. He graduated from the Western Culinary Institute in Portland, Oregon.

Julia: How would you describe how Alaskans think about food? What factors influence our food culture?

Aaron: Definitely seasonal. Seasonality is a huge part of it, and subsistence, too, goes hand in hand with seasonality. The hunting seasons are short, and for a lot of people that's when you fill the freezer. There's dip-netting season and then mountain sheep, moose, caribou seasons kind of overlap, and then that's it. And if you don't have enough put up, you may have to spend a lot of money, which maybe you don't have, at the grocery store. So seasonality, subsistence, necessity, remoteness—all factor in. And, then, are you using what you have? That's huge. We're this landlocked place, and everything that comes to us is from somewhere else, generally speaking. So we have to find a way to manage that access and not waste it because we're paying a premium for it.

Julia: So how do you use Alaskan ingredients?

Aaron: I can think of two really good examples both professionally and privately. Caviar. Caviar is something that has been appreciated for centuries. Alaska was settled by Russians a long time ago before American settlers came,

but after the indigenous people that were here before all of them, and there's still a lot of that influence. I get a ton of fresh fish from local fishermen whenever I can, along with some salmon caviar, and I use it as a garnish on oysters. It's got a great texture.

My uncles and I go out hunting, and if one of us is fortunate to get a moose, we are able to butcher it like a commercial butchery. You can cut these huge beautiful pieces of meat, and then I can turn all the connective tissue into a rich, unctuous, satisfying broth.

Julia: So if you were going to write a cookbook that was really trying to express Alaska's cuisine, what would the elements be?

Aaron: For regular home cooks, I would have a large section on utilizing "waste," like what other people might throw away, for example, how I use the moose bones. And salmon, how to use all the parts of the salmon, like grinding the salmon bones up and composting them, or making bone salt from finely ground salmon bones. One of the driving forces of creativity in Alaska cuisine is making it through the winter. As soon as it's out of the ground or out of the water or out of a tree—whatever—preserving, pickling, canning are important elements. Those activities are a trend going through restaurants. It's kind of a return to a cyclical process. For home cooks, it can be a little daunting but it's not difficult at all. And even if you're just planning on freezing things. I was fortunate to have dinner with my mother the other day and she pulled out green beans that she grew and had blanched and frozen. They were a little bit softer than if they were fresh but the quality was excellent. So that would definitely have to be a part of it.

You and I were talking about doughnuts recently. Some of those recipes that in the fine-dining world, restaurants may have been looked down upon, but that's part of our story. And still if you travel around the state, you'll find that people still love them because they're good.

Julia: Anything else?

Aaron: What does Alaska food mean to me? It means eating with the seasons. It means work. It's a lot of work. It means harvesting, processing, foraging, growing any of those things that you're going to eat. It's better for everyone if we can all eat stuff that grows here, even if it is a struggle. You know, struggle through the winter, struggle to use all of everything. It's about subsistence. It's about sharing. Alaska food is about preservation, in terms of preserving what you catch or harvest or collect in a way that's going to be edible for the upcoming winter. And preserving stories, preserving heritage. Alaska cuisine is about having limited options that force you to be creative, which is healthy and challenging in a really good way.

Sourdough starter, a magical alchemy of flour, water, and yeasts from the air, a food prized for its practicality and utility, might be one of the most perfectly Alaskan foods. My Uncle Tommy O'Malley, who has been nursing along a 100-year-old Juneau strain for the past thirty years, is fond of saying that "sourdoughs" were called that because they slept with their starter to keep it warm, treating it with a tenderness usually reserved for women.

In my weeks of sourdough research, I learned about all kinds of legacy sourdough strains with links to homesteader grandmothers, prospectors' backpacks, and tent city stoves. But the biggest discovery (this is going to be controversial) was this: The story doesn't actually matter. You don't need to use an old sourdough starter passed down through the generations. You can make great pancakes with sourdough starter you just whipped up in your kitchen over the course of two days.

In the old recipe books in the archive at Anchorage Museum, I found that the earliest sourdough pancake recipes, from the 1920s and '30s, don't make a big deal about the provenance of their starters. Turns out, back in the day, pancakes were often just a way to use up old, spent bread starter. (Bread starter is its own project and must be much more active and charged than the starter needed for pancakes.) The sour batter served as a flavor rather than a stand-alone leavening agent. Its acids reacted with baking soda, giving loft to the batter. Vintage recipes also make sourdough sponges (starters) out of all sorts of whole-grain flours, including buckwheat and corn.

According to a 1971 *New York Times* profile of now-deceased Talkeetna sourdough maven "Evil Alice" Powell, you don't need your grandma's starter. "I can make one in forty-eight hours," she told the *Times*. "All it takes is flour, water, sugar, and yeast. You can tell it's ripe by the smell."

A sourdough starter recipe from the classic cookbook *Out of Alaska's Kitchens*, published in 1947, reads:

Take a gallon crock or cookie jar and put in:

2 cups flour
1 teaspoon salt

3 tablespoons sugar

½ teaspoon dry yeast

2 cups lukewarm water

Stir till mixture is a smooth, thin paste. Put on lid and set in a warm place to sour. Stir it several times a day. In two or three days, your sourdough will be ready.

You can also start a crock like Carri Thurman of Two Sisters Bakery in Homer does, with no added yeast, just by submerging a leaf or two of red cabbage in your flour and water paste and removing it after twelve to twenty-four hours when the mixture is bubbling. Cabbage has lots of natural yeast in it.

If you don't want to make starter, many bakeries will give you a cup of starter. I'm a fan of the sourest sourdough for pancakes. A slow, warm ferment can do this. So can using a whole-grain flour in the starter. On the recommendation of Carlyle Watt, executive chef and head baker at Fire Island Rustic Bakeshop, in Anchorage, I tested a starter made with rye flour. It was fantastic, especially with the whole-grain flour in the pancakes.

Another personal preference: I like my pancakes on the thin side, with crêpe-like batter consistency. I thin my batter with plain soda water for extra bubbles, which gives just a little extra loft to the cakes.

I've come up with two sourdough pancake recipes, loosely based on a family recipe from my Uncle Tommy. One recipe is for a traditional white-flour pancake, and another is for a low-gluten, whole-grain version of the pancakes, made with a rye starter, buckwheat, and teff, a naturally sour grain and used for the Ethiopian injera, a sour, spongy flatbread.

SOURDOUGH PANCAKES

SERVES 4 TO 6

At least 12 hours before you want to make your pancakes, make a sponge (starter).

To make the pancake batter, keep the beaten eggs in the refrigerator until ready to cook. Stir the flour, water, sugar, and salt together in a large bowl until smooth. Add the starter and stir to combine. Let sit in a warm place at least 12 hours or as long as 48 hours. When the starter is ready, it should smell sour, be puffy, and be somewhat watery.

Remove the eggs from the refrigerator and bring to room temperature for 30 minutes.

6 eggs, beaten
2 cups white flour, or 1 cup white flour (or Cup4Cup gluten-free flour) and ½ cup buckwheat flour and ½ cup teff flour
1 cup water
⅓ cup sugar
1 teaspoon salt
1 cup sourdough starter (see page 62)
1 stick (½ cup) butter, melted
1½ teaspoons baking soda
Optional: soda water for thinning batter

Put a large skillet over medium heat and heat until nice and hot. With a spatula or wooden spoon, fold the eggs and butter into the starter. Sprinkle the baking soda on the mixture, and stir to combine. You should see the starter gain loft. Thin the batter, if you like, with soda water.

Scoop batter for 4 pancakes into the skillet, and cook for about 2 minutes, until the pancakes have browned on the bottom and have bubbled across the top. Flip and cook for about 30 seconds more. Serve hot on a warm platter with butter and syrup.

VARIATIONS: Experiment by substituting a cup of any combination of flours: buckwheat, whole wheat, teff, corn, rye. If you are trying for gluten-free or low-gluten pancakes, combine a cup of whole-grain flour with a flour mix containing xanthan or guar gum, which acts as a binder, helping the batter trap the bubbles from the starter yeast. You can also make your sponge with buttermilk and, for the sugar, substitute honey, maple syrup, or brown sugar.

Chapter 5

In a City of Strip Malls, a Vietnamese Noodle Revolution

First, eat the pho with your eyes, Tony Chheum told me, when I interviewed him in 2014. Your big, round bowl should be volcanically hot, sending off curls of steam. Next to it, a pile of crisp mung bean sprouts, fresh basil leaves, cilantro sprigs, jalapeño slices, and a wedge of lime awaits. Next to that, if you want, a small platter of thinly cut, extra rare beef.

I was speaking with him in his restaurant, Phonatik, on Dimond. He was sitting across from me at a table in the VIP room, where the graffiti-style artwork on the walls matches his tattoos. I was there to talk about the Vietnamese noodle shops that had been colonizing Anchorage's strip malls.

Drive down any major artery in Anchorage, and a pho shop will eventually appear, tucked in next to a cell phone store or a manicure salon or a dry cleaner. Pho Bowl, Pho 2000, Pho & Grill, Pho Tommy, Pho Jula, Pho Saigon, Pho Vietnams, numbers 1, 2, 3, 4, and 8. As of winter 2018, there were seventeen restaurants in Anchorage with the word *pho* in the name, according to state business licenses.

That's only a sample. It doesn't include Ray's Place in Spenard or any number of Thai restaurants that also serve the noodle soup. You can even

Anchorage residents come from dozens of places around the world. Asian populations—Filipino, Korean, Japanese, Thai, Lao, Hmong, and Vietnamese—are big influences on the local restaurant scene.

Pho, which is plentiful in Anchorage, is served with sides of bean sprouts, lime wedges, and jalapeños. Many restaurants also make their own chili sauce.

get pho in the cafeteria at Providence Alaska Medical Center. The noodle business is deeply competitive. That means pho-eaters have lots of delicious choices, but you have to know what to look for. (Before we go much further, a note on pronunciation: pho is pronounced like the first syllable in "fanatic." It does not rhyme with "bro.")

Phonatik's Tony Chheum, who was twenty-nine when I interviewed him, is a former mechanic from Sacramento, third child of Chinese and Cambodian parents, who grew up working in his family's doughnut shop. Restaurants are in his blood (his sister ran Alaska Bagel Restaurant), and pho, once his favorite hangover food, has been his all-consuming project for the last few years. With the help of his girlfriend, Kimtra Nguyen, and her father, Bung Nguyen, both Vietnamese, he perfected his recipe. His business plan is all about introducing the food to newcomers. He offers first-timers a tableside mini pho-orientation he calls "Pho 101." He took me through it.

"Next," he told me, "eat with your nose. How does it smell?"

Pho done right is built on a broth made from slow-simmered bones. A good bowl should smell herbal, like ginger and star anise layered atop a formidable, beefy aroma. Chheum's broth-making process takes forty-eight hours, he said. He won't talk about the specifics. Few pho-makers do. (Tip: If you have MSG issues, always ask.) A good broth stands on its own, he said. Always taste the broth before adding anything to the bowl.

"A broth should be clean," he said. "It should taste clean. It should be nice and dark."

The noodle soup–selling business is so competitive in Anchorage that every shop has to work to stand out and cultivate regulars. Phonatik holds quarterly soup-eating contests, called "pho challenges," where competitors have thirty minutes to eat as much as they can from eight-pound bowls of noodles, broth, and meat. I went to a ten-way challenge a few months before the interview. The rowdy one-hundred-person crowd of spectators was heavily Hmong and Pacific Islander. The winner, an airport baggage ramp supervisor named Ben Saunoa, went home with $888.

Pho is a distant, Asian cousin of the French beef stew *pot-au-feu* (notice how "feu" sounds like "pho"), and it was born during the French occupation of Vietnam. In some parts of the country, it might be eaten for breakfast or as a bedtime snack. Andrea Nyugen, an Asian food expert and author of the cookbook *Into the Vietnamese Kitchen*, told me what's in your bowl can offer clues about the geographic origins of the recipe. If the broth is on the sweet side and has fried garlic or shallots, then the pho has a Lao or Hmong influence. More greens and a very large bowl is more often served in South Vietnam. In the north, the bowls are smaller and the greens less plentiful, she said.

Chhuem's soups are more traditional Vietnamese and are less sweet. An oily oxtail version is very popular at his shop. At Pho Lena East, my go-to place, soup is done Lao-style, with fried garlic, which is more common in Anchorage. One of Pho Lena's most popular bowls comes with meatballs made with lean beef that is ground in-house. "A lot of Lao people will not eat pho without meatballs," said owner Biponh Morisath-Luce, whose big

A meal at Ray's Place, one of the first restaurants to introduce pho in Anchorage more than twenty years ago. Ray's Place is now located in the Spenard neighborhood.

Lao family owns three pho shops, one on Boniface Parkway, one downtown, and one in Spenard.

Pho has taken off across the United States, but especially in parts of California, Nyugen said. Part of that is driven by Asian immigration, and part of it is because of the wide appeal of this food. "It's easy to eat, it's relatively inexpensive," she said.

Morisath-Luce and Chhuem told me that a combination of things make Anchorage a good market for pho. It's a cold climate, so hot soup has a natural appeal. There is also a big military presence here, and military members tend to be well-traveled, adventurous eaters. The city's diversity helps:

Depending on how you parse the numbers, Asians and Pacific Islanders are now either Anchorage's largest or second largest minority group, behind Alaska Natives. But to say immigrants drive the market would be an over-simplification.

At Phonatik, the regulars come in waves. Late in the evening, when the nail shops close, Vietnamese manicurists come in, Chheum said. On Sunday, after church, it's Samoans, Filipinos, and Koreans. When the bars close, it's a younger, mixed-race crowd. Lunchtime, it's business people from all kinds of backgrounds. The scene inside the shop is a little picture of Anchorage.

The last step in Chheum's Pho 101 is constructing the bite. People have differing opinions about how this should go. Chhuem teaches newbies the "pho shot" technique. Fill your wide spoon with meat, greens, and, possibly, chili sauce. (Chili sauce, made of ground peppers and oil, is its own thing. Many shops in town make their own.) Pho is also often served with Sriracha sauce (hot and garlicky), fish sauce (salty), and hoisin sauce (sweet). Purists say those flavors pollute the broth, kind of like putting ketchup on a gourmet meal, but people can add those sauces to the spoon if they like, Chheum said. Then it goes in your mouth. It should burn just a little. "Chase it with broth," he said. "Then chase that with noodles, kind of like eating bread."

This is how to eat pho if you have some time and want to savor it, he said. Taking time makes it easier to power through the whole gigantic bowl. But pho is essentially fast, warm, comfort food. If you're in a hurry, Chhuem said, just put everything in the bowl (the hot broth cooks the rare beef) and slurp away.

FOOLPROOF WILD BLUEBERRY PIE

SERVES 6

What is it about eating pie from berries you picked yourself in late August, when the coho are running and there's a giant cabbage weigh-off at the fair? Does it taste a little better? Blueberries are one of the most widely available wild berries in Alaska, a subsistence food and a staple of the earliest kitchens. Inky-blue wild berry pie is a quintessential Alaska food.

I come from pie-making people. My Uncle Tommy, a pie-baking champion from Girdwood, is known in certain circles as "His Pieness." I'm not a gifted pie baker despite watching great pies being baked a thousand times. But, still, I was determined to write a recipe that is both awesome and hard to mess up for those not naturally inclined. Every Alaska cook should have a pie recipe up their sleeve. And this is now mine.

This one has two unorthodox aspects. The first is that I make the crust using a food processor. Tommy would never approve, but when I do it in the processor, I just like the dough better. The flour and fat get mixed really well without the warmth of your hands to make the fat soft. (You can also mix the fat and flour into a fine meal by hand, pioneer style. There are people who swear by it.) The second, which comes straight from His Pieness, is that I use tapioca flour to thicken it. Bob's Red Mill's tapioca flour is available in a number of grocery stores in Anchorage. It makes the pie set up just right. But, of course, that means waiting for it to cool. You can also use cornstarch, regular tapioca, potato starch, arrowroot, or flour. Fat-wise, my family has a longstanding debate going about lard/Crisco versus butter, and this recipe splits the difference. Oh, and one last thing: You

FOR THE PASTRY:

2 cups flour

2 tablespoons sugar

½ teaspoon salt

1½ sticks (12 ounces) cold salted butter, cut into slices

½ cup cold Crisco shortening

4 to 6 tablespoons ice water or ice-cold vodka

One egg, lightly beaten

FOR THE FILLING:

4 to 5 cups wild blueberries, picked over for stems/leaves/spiders

1 cup sugar

⅓ cup tapioca flour

Zest of ½ lemon

can use ice-cold vodka instead of water in the crust if you like. It makes the crust flakier.

FOR THE PASTRY: At least three hours before your planned pie-eating time, make the pastry: In the bowl of a food processor (or blender), add the flour, sugar, and salt, and pulse to combine. Then add the butter and Crisco, and pulse until a fine meal forms. Slowly add the ice water or vodka, 1 tablespoon at a time, and pulse, occasionally scraping down the side of the bowl with a spatula, until the pastry comes together and forms a ball.

Using a spatula, scrape out the dough onto a lightly floured work surface. Separate into 2 slightly flattened rounds, wrap in plastic wrap, and refrigerate. Chill for at least 2 hours. Keep the beaten egg in the refrigerator until using.

FOR THE FILLING: Meanwhile, in a large bowl, put the blueberries, sugar, tapioca flour, and lemon zest and mix until well combined. If you like, let the filling mixture macerate (soften and become juicy) while the dough chills.

When you're ready to make the pie, preheat the oven to 350°F, and get out a standard 9-inch pie dish.

On the lightly floured work surface with a floured rolling pin, roll out one of the pastry rounds for the bottom crust. Gently fold it in half and in half again, lift it into the pie pan, unfold it, and press it gently into the pie pan.

Stir the berry mixture, and spoon it into the bottom crust evenly. Roll out the top crust, leaving about ½ inch extra around the edge for sealing the edges. Crimp the bottom and top crust edges together with your fingers to seal. With a small sharp knife, cut 3 or 4 slits in the top crust to let steam escape.

Brush the top crust with the beaten egg. Set the pie pan on a sheet pan to catch any overflow.

Bake for 1 hour and then have a look at the pie. The filling should be bubbling out of the top crust vents and the crust should be golden. It may need as much as 10 minutes more baking time.

Transfer the pie to a cooling rack for a half hour at least. The pie will set as it cools (if you can wait that long). To serve, cut into wedges and top with a scoop of vanilla ice cream.

Chapter 6

Free Alaskan Salmon: Just Bring a Net and Expect a Crowd

Wenceslous Fru, a physician's assistant from Anchorage, stood on the sandy shore of the Kenai River and imagined the dinner he would put together once he felt the jostle of a salmon in his long-handled dip net. He would make it the way they do back home in Cameroon, splitting it down the belly and opening it like a book, rubbing it with ginger, garlic, and spices, and then slipping it under the broiler.

Fishing nearby in the summer of 2017, Raviwan Dougherty, an Anchorage restaurant worker from Thailand, envisioned steaming hers and bathing it in fish sauce, lime juice, and chiles. Lyubov Miroshnick, who works in a dental office in Wasilla, planned to smoke her catch after soaking it in her Ukrainian grandparents' brine recipe. "Mainly, we fish for the winter," said Ms. Miroshnick, who had a dozen family members with her. "That's how most people survive here. It's the cheaper way."

There is no more popular fishery in Alaska than the Kenai River, a three-hour drive southwest of Anchorage, where millions of sockeye salmon ripple through the silty turquoise water each summer to spawn. And there is most likely no more democratic fishing spot in America—a place where any Alaska

FOLLOWING: Fishermen pose with their catch on the bank of the Kenai River. Dipnetting for red salmon is a common, lower-cost way people in Anchorage get fish to fill their freezers.

resident, from an oil company executive to a carwash attendant, can fill a freezer with premium salmon for only the cost of gas and gear.

Most of the Kenai's fish are caught by commercial boats and sold around the world. The rest go to sport fishermen, who catch them with a rod and reel, and, increasingly, a widely diverse group of mostly urban dipnetters, who crowd the river's mouth for three weeks in July, hoping to score a winter's supply of wild salmon that most can't afford to buy. In the roughly twenty years since the state started regulating dip-net fishing in the region, the number of permits issued has doubled, to more than thirty thousand.

Now, when the dipnetters descend, the beach takes on the motley, slightly claustrophobic feel of a music festival. Whole families set up camp on the sand, hauling tents, chairs, dogs, children, and nets by four-wheelers from the packed parking lot. One year, a church group brought in a bouncy house and grilled hot dogs. A cart sold espresso. People on the beach spoke Hmong, Korean, Tagalog, Spanish, and Thai. They played Christian rock, reggaeton, and Pacific Island R&B.

July's dip-net army lifts the economy in the town of Kenai, but it also clogs the highway and litters the beach with fish heads and guts that have to be raked to the water at night by special tractors. Hundreds of gulls cry overhead, diving to feast on entrails. On weekends, when crowding is at its worst, there are dustups over fishing territory, tangled gear, pilfered bags of ice, and stolen coolers. Differences in culture, language, and notions of personal space sometimes fuel the conflicts.

"It used to be two-hundred people—now it's five thousand!" on a given day, said Scott Turney, an Anchorage telecommunications engineer who has been fishing on the river's beach for more than thirty years. "There never used to be any conflicts, but the newcomers don't have the same courtesy. As soon as you drag a fish out, one or two people will come take your place." Even with the crowds, he said, landing a big haul of fish is worth the hassle: "I still love it. I'll never stop."

To fish, most people stand elbow to elbow along the shoreline, wearing waders, chest-high in the cold river. Each holds a long steel pole with a five-foot-wide net basket on the end. When a fish hits the net, the fisher drags it onto the beach and bonks it on the head with a short bat. Some people also fish by boat to avoid the crowd, holding their nets overboard as they drift with the current.

A fisherman shakes a red salmon from his dip net on the beach next to the Kenai River.

Occasionally, a commercial boat putters by. There's always a little tension. Commercial fishermen catch salmon by stretching large nets in the inlet at the outside edge of the mouth of the river. When things are slow, dipnetters grumble that the larger boats take too many fish. The commercial fishermen, on the other hand, must sometimes stop work for a few days at the direction of state biologists who monitor the number of fish in the river for conservation purposes. They don't love watching the dipnetters filling their coolers. "It's always hard to not be catching fish," said Hannah Heimbuch, who runs a thirty-two-foot aluminum commercial boat, *Salmon Slut*, in the inlet. "I feel like our harvest is pretty responsible and pretty moderate."

A single dipnetter is allowed to take home twenty-five sockeye, or red, salmon, and an additional ten for each family member per season—limits

Sina Tulimasealii cleans fish to be shared with members of her church in Anchorage.

are enforced by state officers who patrol the beach. The average dip-net fisher in Cook Inlet—the 180-mile finger of ocean that runs along the Kenai Peninsula from Anchorage to the Gulf of Alaska—brings home sixty to seventy pounds of salmon each summer, said Ricky Gease, the executive director of the Kenai River Sportfishing Association. Even in Alaska, this is a bargain: Although wild salmon can sell for more than twenty-five dollars a pound in the Lower 48, here it will still cost ten dollars or more at the grocery.

An estimated 90,000 people, fishers and their families, share about 400,000 sockeye annually, Mr. Gease said, which breaks down to 2.4 million meals, the majority of fish coming from the Kenai. Food bank workers in Anchorage say salmon has also become a supplemental source of protein for the city's hungry. "Outside the revenues generated from oil," Mr. Gease said, "this is the largest single shared natural resource in Alaska for residents."

Over the years, the town has become better at managing the parking, the trash, and the fish waste. The number of dip-netting permits issued has dropped a bit in the past few years, leading to speculation that the fishery has reached its saturation point.

On July 29, on the last weekend of the season, fishers lined up in the sun under a noisy tangle of gulls. Sina Tulimasealii, wearing a protective skirt made from a garbage bag, cleaned salmon on top of a plastic container, a coral-colored heap of roe at her feet. She planned to bake her fish with mayonnaise, lemon pepper, and green onion, she said. Her Anchorage church, Manai Fou Assembly of God, holds services in Samoan.

About thirty church members were catching fish that day to share with the congregation. Working in community to share, especially with elders, is a Samoan cultural value, she said, similar to the Alaska Native subsistence values about sharing and caring for elders. Her group used the Samoan word *mafutaga*—fellowship—to describe what it feels like to be on the beach with so many people. "Some of our elders cannot fish, so we fish for them," Ms. Tulimasealii said. "It's not all about fishing, though. It's about having fun."

MAKES ABOUT 2 CUPS

When I thought about writing a recipe for smoked salmon spread, I got all nostalgic about my Aunt Alicia's recipe. I could picture it, set out before family dinner on a Sunday, in the ceramic bowl on a plate stacked with Wheat Thins. My uncle Bob, who dipnetted the Copper River for salmon, was our family's main salmon supplier. Alicia was an expert with the backyard Little Chief smoker. I immediately texted my cousin to ask for the recipe.

> Can I have your mom's salmon spread recipe?

> Oddly, I think all she did was take her smoked salmon that was too salty and mix it with cream cheese.

> No green onions?

> Maybe sometimes and capers too.

And that's when I remembered Rule No. 1 about Alaska cooking: We are always adapting to what we have on hand. What do we have at the cabin? What's in the freezer? What could we get at the store? Do we have leftover grilled salmon? Did the smoked salmon come out a little salty?

I settled on a basic recipe for the spread, and a crowd-sourced, choose-your-own-adventure list of things to add, in keeping with how most people seem to like salmon spread.

Here's what's cookin' SALMON PARTY LOG Serves
Recipe from the kitchen of Audrey
1# tin salmon (2 c.)
8 oz cream cheese
1 T. lemon juice
2 t. grated onion
2 T. prepared horseradish
¼ t. salt
¼ t. liquid smoke (delete if
3 T. ch. parsley   ½ c. pecans (optional)
...in salmon, mix in next 6 ingredients.
...Can be rolled in ch. parsley + nuts.

A good base spread has a nice mix of fat, brine, acid, and onion (heat is optional, but I'm a big fan of Frank's RedHot sauce in the base).

For the spread, much depends on the flavor of the fish. A particular thing to pay attention to is the sweetness. I find the sweeter smoked fish works really well when you want to make your spread on the hotter side. Just don't forget to tell the kids it has a kick.

I like whipped cream cheese for the base because it spreads well on crackers, though a person could use a mix of traditional cream cheese and sour cream for the same effect. If you want to add in Asian flavors like Sriracha or wasabi, I think the result will taste better if you sub in mayo for half the cream cheese. The consistency is a little more dip-like and works great in the center of a sushi roll. For mayo, you might try Kewpie mayonnaise, available at most Asian markets; it contains MSG but also really packs in the umami flavor. For smoked salmon spread, I like green onions better than grated onion, onion powder, or seasoned salt (but, if you're camping, onion salt works well.).

1 cup (about 7 ounces) flaked smoked salmon, or mix of smoked salmon and leftover grilled salmon
1 cup (8 ounces) whipped cream cheese
Juice and zest of ½ lemon
¼ cup finely chopped green onion
Salt
Freshly ground black pepper

My favorite party smoked salmon spread recipe, adapted from the recipe given to me by Steve Kruschwitz, who edits the technical parts of the food newsletter at the *Anchorage Daily News*, is the following base spread with an additional 8 finely chopped pickled jalapeño rounds, 2 tablespoons jalapeño brine, and ½ super finely chopped fresh jalapeño.

Mix all ingredients until combined. If you like the dip really smooth, whiz it in a food processor (or blender).

Other add-ins to consider are:
- Up to 1 tablespoon prepared horseradish
- 2 to 3 dashes Frank's RedHot sauce or Tabasco sauce
- 1 to 2 tablespoons sweet pickle relish
- Generous shake of seasoned salt
- 8 to 10 pickled jalapeño chiles (plus a splash of the brine)
- 1 finely chopped fresh jalapeño
- 2 tablespoons capers (plus a splash of the brine)
- Up to 1 tablespoon Sriracha sauce (substitute mayonnaise for half the cream cheese)
- 2 teaspoons prepared wasabi (substitute mayonnaise for half the cream cheese)

Chapter 7

How Spam Musubi Edged Its Way into Anchorage's Food Scene

Kenji Kusano never measures. For a lifelong Japanese chef, the ratio of water to rice comes ingrained like the lines on the palm of your hand. On this particular day, in the kitchen of the split-level house he shares with his wife, Sandy, he rinsed the milky starch out of a few cups of Calrose rice. Soon he'd make a favorite fishing snack: Spam musubi. It's rice sandwiched around fried Spam, wrapped in seaweed and then plastic wrap. Perfect for a jacket pocket.

Now seventy-two, Kusano has rolled more sushi than just about anybody in Anchorage. He helped open what may have been Anchorage's first sushi bar, at Tempura Kitchen, in the early 1980s. Then came Yamato Ya, a sushi institution he owned for twenty-five years. At first, his clientele comprised a handful of Japanese airline workers. By the time he retired, the California roll was everywhere in town. "The grocery store. The mall," he said.

Kusano explained that like sushi, pad Thai, and pho before it, musubi, a Japanese-influenced Hawaiian snack, has edged deeply into Alaska's mainstream food culture. Sandy, who grew up in Hawaii, has been following the trend. "They sell it at the gas station now," she said.

Chances are, if you're in Anchorage, you're not far from a piece of musubi. Find it at a half-dozen restaurants, at church picnics, and football practices.

It's available by the piece at New Sagaya stores and at Chevron stations with the Pall Malls and 5-Hour Energy shots. It never costs more than three dollars.

Sometimes food can be a carrier molecule for the story of a place. A meal of wild salmon might carry the story of how a family fishes every year. A paper plate of sliced, salted muktuk (the skin and blubber of a whale), eaten at a kitchen table in Anchorage, might carry the story of a faraway village, a family, and a culture.

Musubi tells us something about Alaska history and culture too. Start with Spam (a canned, processed meat first introduced in 1937), a familiar flavor for lots of Alaskans. Spam's rise in popularity also followed the military, which served it to soldiers beginning in World War II, according to Spam's official website. Alaska has always been a popular destination for veterans, and their familiarity with Spam likely influenced everybody's palate. (Alaska still has more vets per capita—12 percent of the population—than any other state.)

Musubi also gets into Alaska's deep relationship with Hawaii and the Pacific Islands. Hawaii is a popular vacation spot, a direct flight away. Alaska also has more Pacific Islanders per capita than any other state besides Hawaii, according to US Census data, but the numbers are small, maybe 2 percent of the population. That seeds a base market.

But the demand for musubi goes far beyond Islanders, said Corinna Kanaina, general manager of the Hula Hands Hawaiian restaurants. Hula Hands has been selling musubi for eighteen years, she said. Recently, sales have shot up. So far this year, the restaurant's two Anchorage locations have sold nearly nine thousand pieces, four times what they sold in 2014. They have orders for hundreds of musubi at once now, for business conferences and football jamborees.

Spam's taste fits well with the flavors of Polynesian cuisine, she said. (Hawaii, according to Spam corporate, has the highest Spam consumption in America.) "I think it's just the taste, the salty, pork, bacon-type of taste," said Kanaina.

Musubi is ripe for variations. Some places add egg or teriyaki chicken. Kenji likes to experiment with ingredients that riff on popular sandwiches, appealing to American tastebuds. On the day he was cooking, he took slices of ham and American cheese, dunked them in tempura batter, rolled them in

Musubi, including Spam Musubi, prepared in Kenji and Sandy Kusano's kitchen

Sandy Kusano shows off her Spam Musubi.

panko, and deep-fried them, then added lettuce to make a musubi ham and cheese sandwich.

The savory taste of Spam musubi also appeals to the wide variety of Asian palates in Anchorage, Kanaina said. Koreans, for example, eat a sushi roll made with pickled vegetables and ham or Spam called kimbop. Filipinos, who represent the largest share of the city's Asian population, make a number of dishes that rely on salty pork and rice. Sandy Kusano remembers that she first started eating Spam at home in the 1960s. It was a natural addition to a variety of onigiri, or Japanese rice balls, sometimes filled with meat or seafood and wrapped in rice that they already ate as a family.

"I think a lot of the Alaska Natives have picked up on not just the taste, but we are close in culture when it comes to the sea, the seaweed," she said. Hula Hands's recipe is traditional, she said, with two slices of deep-fried Spam splashed with their special teriyaki sauce, between plain short-grain Japanese rice, wrapped in nori (sheets of dried seaweed). The Chevron gas station version is a different style that uses a smaller strip of nori and combines the rice with Furikake, a dry Japanese rice seasoning.

Brandon Mahi, manager at Kansha, a Japanese and Hawaiian restaurant in South Anchorage, said he's also seen an uptick in interest in musubi. Its popularity with the military crowd surprised him at first, he said, but it makes sense. Military people are well-traveled and many have spent time in Hawaii. The flavor is comforting and nostalgic for a lot of different kinds of people in Alaska. "Everybody just kinda likes Spam sometimes."

SPAM MUSUBI AND THE MUSUBI MCMUFFIN

MAKES ROUGHLY 10 MUSUBI SNACKS

Spam Musubi is a simple, portable, savory snack of Spam, rice, nori (dried seaweed) sheets, and selected other ingredients. Many Alaskans, especially those of us with Hawaiian connections and those who grew up in rural Alaska villages, have a nostalgic soft spot for the taste of Spam, which became widely popular during WWII when fresh meat was rationed. Spam is available in several flavored versions, but for this recipe, I use the low-sodium kind. Musubi is a Hawaiian take on onigiri, or Japanese rice balls, which come in numerous shapes with different fillings.

According to Kenji Kusano, one of Anchorage's best known sushi chefs, and his wife, Sandy, who was raised in Hawaii, the hardest part of making musubi is getting the rice just right. They insist on rinsing the rice well and soaking it before cooking it in a rice cooker. (An electric rice cooker is indispensable for making perfect rice, and is not very expensive. Cooking rice on the stovetop is more challenging, but Chef Kusano offers instructions for that method, following.) According to Sandy, the traditional method of making musubi is to use unflavored rice and to fry the Spam slices. She buys the forms for making musubi in Hawaii, and says Walmart in Anchorage has the best, cheapest rice and nori. To make the musubi, you will need a musubi form (available at Asian groceries or on Amazon for about seven dollars). Or you can use a rinsed Spam can, cut with a can opener on the bottom edge, but watch those sharp edges.

A useful tip from Hula Hands, a Hawaiian restaurant that has been selling musubi in Anchorage for at least eighteen years, is to pay close attention to the temperature of the ingredients while you are working with them, keeping the rice and Spam as warm as possible and immediately wrapping the musubi in plastic wrap to keep the moisture in and soften the nori. Hand-roll-size nori sheets are available at some Asian groceries and on

3 cups Calrose rice, rinsed well, and soaked for 45 minutes to 1 hour

1 package hand-roll-size nori seaweed sheets

1 (12-ounce) can reduced-sodium Spam, sliced thinly into 10 pieces

Optional: Teriyaki sauce, Furikake rice seasoning (available at Asian markets)

Amazon. Regular sheets will also work, but you will need to cut them to size with sharp scissors.

Chef Kusano made me a very tasty musubi version of a ham and cheese sandwich, with lettuce and a tempura-battered fried ham pocket full of American cheese. That led me to experiment with sandwich fixings. My favorite was a musubi version of a breakfast sandwich, like a drive-through Egg McMuffin in all its melty American-cheese glory. It's not health food, but it's delicious.

Cook the rice according to package directions and keep warm in the rice cooker. (If you desire, season the rice with Furikake seasoning and mix well. This is how they do it at Chevron.)

Place the 10 pieces of SPAM into a large frying pan (no oil necessary) and cook over medium heat until golden brown on both sides.

Wet the musubi form and set it on a damp plate. Firmly fill the form a little less than halfway with cooked rice. Layer with a slice of fried Spam and, if desired, a splash of teriyaki sauce.

Firmly fill the form the rest of the way with rice. Press gently with the plunger to compact. While pressing the plunger with one hand, slide the form up with the other to free the musubi. Carefully peel the plunger from the top layer of rice (a sharp knife can help if it sticks; remember to keep it wet).

Roll the shaped rice and Spam tightly in a slice of nori, and wrap in plastic wrap right away.

Ideally, serve warm. When ready to serve, slice the wrapped musubi in half with a serrated knife. Spam musubi keeps, well wrapped, for a day at room temperature.

MCMUFFIN MUSUBI

You'll need all the previously listed ingredients, as well as:
3 eggs, well beaten
Olive oil
5 slices American cheese singles
Optional: Gochujang, Frank's RedHot sauce, Tabasco sauce, or Sriracha
    sauce

Coat a medium frying pan with a generous layer of olive oil and heat over medium-low heat. When the pan is hot, pour in the eggs to form a thin layer. Cook for about 5 minutes, until just set. Turn off the heat and allow the eggs to cool and firm up in the pan on the stove for 3 to 5 more minutes.

Transfer the cooked eggs in one piece with a spatula to a cutting board. Using the plunger of the musubi form as a guide, cut the egg into rectangles using kitchen shears or a sharp knife.

Cut the American cheese singles in half. Following the instructions for making musubi, then to each add a layer of American cheese, egg, and a squirt of hot sauce.

The warm Spam and rice will melt the cheese. Serve immediately.

KENJI KUSANO'S STOVETOP MUSUBI RICE

Rinse 3 cups Japanese short-grain rice. Put it in a large bowl, cover with water, stir in a circular motion, and replace the water 4 or 5 times, until it runs clear. Once rinsed, leave the rice to soak in a bowl for 45 minutes to an hour. Drain the rice.

Put the rice in a large pot with 3 cups of water over medium heat, covered with a tight lid, and bring to a boil. Turn the heat down to low, and set a timer to 15 minutes. When the timer goes off, remove the lid: the water should be mostly absorbed. Turn the heat to high for up to 30 seconds, until you can hear the rice crackle on the bottom of the pan.

Turn off the heat, and leave the pot on the stove, covered (this is essential), for 15 minutes. Do not remove the lid.

Chapter 8

Thirty Days of Muktuk

The thirty-day whale diet started as a joke. It was Christmastime 2016 and Josh Ahsoak's sister, AnnaFlora, was visiting him in Anchorage. She was doing a thirty-day CrossFit diet and was trying to get him to join her. He wasn't sold on her regimen, but it did make him think. "I had a bunch of life stuff I was dealing with, including trying to get my health and my weight under control," he said.

Josh Ahsoak, thirty-eight, is an Anchorage-based attorney by vocation. By avocation, he's a hunter. Ahsoak is Inupiat, with roots in Utqiagvik (Barrow), where he is on his family's whaling crew. He travels frequently in the state, and estimates he spends about a third of the year subsistence hunting and fishing. As his sister listed her new dietary restrictions, his thoughts turned to his freezer and the array of wild food inside: fish, birds, seal, walrus, bowhead. "At any given time, I will have anywhere between 50 and 500 pounds of just incredibly good meat and fish on hand from all the hunting and fishing activities," he said. What would happen, he wondered, if he switched to a traditional Alaska Native diet for a month?

A northern indigenous diet is centered on marine mammal protein and edible plants. What if he focused on the freezer and avoided eating out or eating processed foods? Ahsoak settled on whale meat, or muktuk, as the main protein in his diet. He had plenty from a successful spring hunt in Barrow. Whale is also high in vitamins D and C, low in carbohydrate, and nutrient dense. Hunters eat it before going out because it is said to give

Josh Ahsoak uses an ulu to cut whale skin and blubber in his downtown Anchorage kitchen.

them energy and keep them warmer. Ahsoak used to eat it in law school before taking long exams because, he said, it kept him from getting hungry. "It takes your body so long to digest it, it's kind of like the opposite of some kind of empty carb or empty sugar," he said. "You don't eat a lot, that's the biggest thing. It's very filling."

And so it began. His sister did her diet, and he ate about eight to ten ounces of whale daily. Usually at lunch with a salad. He also added it to fried rice and made it into spring rolls. He exercised moderately. Soon he quit feeling hungry for breakfast. At night, he ate only a snack. "I would have to remind myself to eat at like seven or eight," he said.

Ahsoak chronicled his meals on Facebook like someone on a trendy diet, using the hashtag #30daymaktakchallenge. His friends, Native and non-Native, cheered him on. By the end of the month, he'd lost seventeen pounds. "I felt much better physically and emotionally when I was eating well," he said.

Whale is often cut on cardboard, which holds up to the blade of an ulu or knife, absorbs odiferous oil, and can be easily discarded.

Gary Ferguson, chief executive officer at the Rural Alaska Community Action Program, Inc. (RurAL CAP), and a naturopathic doctor who has long been involved with nutrition in Alaska Native communities, said Ahsoak's experience fits what doctors know about traditional diets and the metabolic hardwiring of some Alaska Natives. Alaska Natives, who historically did not eat sugar or refined carbohydrates, have a higher chance of having a genetic propensity toward difficulties digesting those foods, he said.

"I find that folks who eat a more traditional diet—healthy proteins, healthy fats, and less grains and processed carbohydrates—they do better," he said. Traditional diets are associated with lower blood sugar levels and reduced risk for cardiovascular disease, he said. Proteins take longer to digest and fats make people feel sated.

For Alaska Native people living in the urban world without as much access to traditional foods, trying to eat a diet high in proteins like fish and good fats like olive oil, and low in sugars and carbs can be really beneficial, he said. "Even at restaurants, start thinking through the eyes of our ancestors. Order the types of food they ate."

His month-long eating experience also made Ahsoak reflect on the cultural value of subsistence, he said. He lived in Barrow until he was six, and then moved to Michigan with his mother. He didn't return to the village until he was nineteen. "There was a lot of things I kind of had to catch up on," he said, referring to when he returned to the village.

He recalled a hunt with his father when he first came back to the village. They went on foot looking for birds and shot as many as they could carry, he said. "I remember thinking, okay, we're not going to have to go hunting for a while, this is enough," he said. He figured they would fill their own freezers, but then they returned to the village and he saw that his dad wasn't thinking that way.

"We went back to my grandfather's house and he stuck his head in the door and held up a duck and my grandfather was sitting on the couch. He looked up, nodded," he said. "We went in just concentric circles out from there to relatives and elderly, and we got maybe three blocks till we got to the one extra duck that we kept." And that was when he understood the dramatic difference between hunting culture and subsistence, he said. Hunters hunt for themselves. "Subsistence means you are hunting for a community."

When he's prepping up subsistence foods like salmon, he often posts pictures on Facebook. Friends from out of state will ask if they can buy some. "I have to explain that I'm not opposed to the idea of sending them salmon, but culturally, I can't [sell] it," he said. "I'll get bagels and things from people in New York, and I'll send them salmon and that's how it works." Or he just sends them salmon. "Subsistence isn't about reciprocity," he said.

Recently Ahsoak was in New York and got to thinking about the hipster trend of elevating old-fashioned objects and foods, glorifying the wearing of flannel, making axes into wall art, calling a jar of pickles "artisan." "There is this searching for authenticity, even if it is your damn pickle next to your white bread sandwich," he said.

Whatever it is that those people seem to be looking for, he said, Alaska has it naturally, when it comes to abundant wild foods. With whale, a whole community comes together to harvest, and values it as part of a system that allows people to live in the Arctic. Unlike something processed on a store shelf, it's a food rooted in a value system and a place.

"Unless you're being deliberate about it, it's easy to fall into a life where you're not eating anything that's been made with any care. You become divorced from your food," he said. "When I hold a fish in my hand and gill it and gut it and put in the box, I'm getting as close as I can to the food. I can say I know where this fish came from because I took it out of the water. I think that's the definition of authenticity."

Gary Ferguson
ALEUT NATUROPATHIC DOCTOR

Gary Ferguson is a naturopathic doctor who is Aleut/Unangan. He grew up in Sand Point, in the Aleutian Islands region of Alaska. He now lives in Anchorage, where he has for many years been involved with Alaska Native health and nutrition, advocating for traditional foods and a return to traditional diets as a way to combat common health concerns like diabetes. He is very familiar with the distinct contrasts and tensions at the center of Alaska's food culture between modern shelf-stable foods and ancient wild foods. He also knows the many ethnic and cultural influences from immigrants that shape Alaska's eclectic cooking culture, especially in the urban part of the state.

Julia: What are the things that make it challenging to find healthy foods in villages?

Gary: In our rural communities, especially, it's really difficult to eat healthy. At least the perception is it's hard to eat healthy because we think of eating out of the local store, especially shelf-stable items. Often those aren't the best foods for us because they have lots of preservatives and their nutrition profile isn't so good.

Traditionally, of course, we ate more from the store outside the door, eating healthier and living off the land: hunting, fishing, gathering, and growing our own food. But now, many people eat out of a local store, choosing DiGiorno's Pizza or Hot Pockets or other prepared foods that are quick to fix and have become the norm. People are saying, I can't eat healthy, because they're thinking about the local store, rather than connecting with the environment and learning from the folks in our communities that are the hunters, fishers, and gatherers. I feel like the subsistence way is the true culture of our rural communities: the sharing, and what you don't get for yourself is shared with you, and then in turn you share the bounty of what you have. I feel like that's the heartbeat of how we used to live traditionally, and it extended to Native and non-Native peoples alike.

Some of our communities in the Aleutian region—Akutan, for example—are still living the old way. I was just out there recently, and when I arrived they had silver salmon that was freshly caught. Everyone brought down a bag or bucket and got some fish. And there was a seal that they had just harvested and fresh seal meat was on the beach, as well as halibut. I feel like there are lessons to be learned from sharing. Many of us who have had urban experiences are used to living out of the store and not relying on the environment and our neighbors for food. As we look to the future, I think we need to reinvigorate the practices of sharing and bartering.

Julia: What have you learned about the traditional Alaska Native diet and what happens if people choose to follow that?

Gary: I spend a lot of my career working with Alaska Native populations, regarding tribal health and diabetes prevention. Diabetes is often connected to our lifestyle and how we eat, and whether we have healthier foods available and the healthy lifestyles that go with getting those foods. Traditionally our Alaska Native diet was of the environment. We had healthy proteins such as land animals or sea animals; we had fish and we had berries and roots that were major parts of our traditional diet. It was very simple, but very nutritious at the same time, and we had recipes that came from ingredients we found locally. We know that the traditional diet is healthier for Alaska Native people and it's probably healthier for everyone else as well. Studies show that Native people who eat a traditional diet, such as seal and salmon and the healthy fats that come from these animals, have less cardiovascular disease, less diabetes and pre-diabetes.

Julia: Where does climate change fit in terms of how people can experience a traditional lifestyle?

Gary: As I've traveled the state working with our peoples in our urban and rural communities, I see huge changes in our climate. Climate change has caused disruptions in animal migration patterns. It has caused changes in when our salmon show up in streams to spawn, because of the longer summer weather and the warming of streams. The salmon runs are now often later. And that's affected our commercial fishermen as well as our subsistence fishers and our gathering customs.

Recently I was talking with an elder in Southeast Alaska and he mentioned how the salmonberries now are ripe two months earlier than when he was a child. And so when we look at our berry harvests and the changing terrain, some berries are actually more prolific due to climate change and others are less available because it's too dry or too wet. We are all going to have to come together to address how the changing climate patterns relate to our food-gathering systems.

Climate change is also affecting the way we gather our foods because there are more vigorous storms. During the winters, we've got less ice for subsistence gatherers to travel on, and our routes for accessing traditional food sources are changing. There are also new dangers related to going out, whereas in the past it used to be just easy to get on your snowmobile or your boat to go out in the ocean. Now there are larger bodies of water that are open because the ice pack is melting, creating dangers for hunters and fishers.

Julia: How would you define Alaska cuisine?

Gary: Alaska now has one of the most eclectic cuisines in the world. It's built on so many different cultures that have come to the state, starting with our Alaska Native cultures that evolved over time, and then with the arrival of European and Russian cuisines. So we've got recipes that are traditional and some that are modern. Recently we've got an infusion of Latino and Mexican and Asian cuisines in our state. So you see moose tacos and different versions of geoduck, and Eskimo ice cream with different ingredients, and it's exciting to see all this variety.

SERVES 4

Tracking the DNA of the classic Alaska baked fish dish with cream sauce, Halibut Olympia, took me down some cool rabbit holes related to the advent of power generation in Alaska (beginning in the late nineteenth century), the history of jarred mayonnaise (Best Foods mayonnaise on the West Coast and Hellmann's east of the Mississippi, which was in wide circulation by the late 1920s), and the spread of refrigeration into rural areas in the United States (mostly after 1935).

Baked Halibut is mentioned in Alaska's cookbooks from the early part of the twentieth century, but in those recipes it's usually cooked with tomato sauce. Canned tomatoes were shelf-stable and pretty much widely available, and they figure in lots of recipes.

The earliest recipe I could find that calls for baking fish in a cream sauce is an undated early twentieth-century cookbook in the Anchorage Museum collection, *Cook Book*, compiled by The Friendly Aid Society of the First Presbyterian Church in Anchorage. That recipe, contributed by Mrs. H. W. Nagley, whose husband owned the general store in Talkeetna, was written for canned tuna, and calls for a homemade white sauce covered with "buttered crumbs or grated cheese." A person could say it was also an early relative of tuna-noodle casserole (which appeared in many Alaska cookbooks from the mid-twentieth century on, likely also related to the shelf-stable, affordable nature of canned tuna).

Halibut Olympia–type dishes began to appear in lots of cookbooks after World War II. By then, refrigeration was widely available. Recipes collected

About 2 pounds fresh halibut, cut into 4 to 6 serving-size pieces

2 tablespoons salt, plus 2 teaspoons

2 to 3 cups white wine

2 tablespoons butter, at room temperature

½ cup sour cream

½ cup mayonnaise

¼ cup grated Parmesan cheese, plus 2 tablespoons

Zest of ½ lemon

2 dashes Tabasco sauce (optional)

¼ large white onion, grated

½ teaspoon Dijon mustard

Ritz crackers (about two per serving), crushed

in church cookbooks also began to show the influence of brands, like Best
Foods, which was mentioned by name in a number of early baked halibut
recipes.

In the Anchorage Women's Club cookbook, *Alaska's Cooking*, published
in 1959, a cook identified as Mrs. John C. Tower recommended broiling halibut with mayonnaise ("must be Best Foods," she writes), lemon, and finely
chopped onion.

Halibut Olympia has come down to us in all kinds of regional variations.
There's Halibut Caddy Ganty from Southeast Alaska, made with wine-
soaked fish, rolled in bread crumbs, covered with mayo, sour cream, and
chopped onion (there's a fine recipe for that dish in *A Collection of Recipes
from Gustavus Inn*, published in 1973, a cookbook every Alaska cook should
own). There's Halibut Alyeska, which I suspect is a pipeline-era dish, made
with grated Cheddar cheese on top and sautéed onions on the bottom.
There's Halibut Sitka, made with chopped green onions in the mayonnaise
sauce.

The following recipe hits on the notes of many historic recipes I've come
across and is influenced heavily by the dish I ate as a kid. (I like to think,
though, that it's just a little better.)

At least two hours before dinner, lay out the halibut in a large shallow bowl, generously season with the 2 tablespoons salt, and cover with the wine. About a half-hour before dinner, preheat the oven to 500°F. Generously butter a baking pan.

To prepare the sauce, whisk together the sour cream, mayonnaise, the ¼ cup grated Parmesan cheese, lemon zest, Tabasco sauce (if using), onion, and mustard. Season with the remaining 2 teaspoons salt.

Remove the fish from the wine and dry well with paper towels. Place the fish in the prepared pan, spread each piece with some of the sauce, and sprinkle with the cracker crumbs and the remaining 2 tablespoons Parmesan cheese.

Bake for about 15 minutes, until the center of the thickest fish piece is still just a little translucent and the crackers have browned. Remove to a cooling rack for 10 minutes (the fish will continue to cook for a few minutes). Serve hot.

Chapter 9

Eating Well at the End of the Road

In the beginning, when Emily was teaching herself to slaughter and butcher, she sequestered the animal before delivering a bullet to its brain. She thought it would be more respectful to let it face its end privately. Plus, there were the feelings of the other pigs to consider. What would it do to them to see one of their own go out by gunshot? It turned out that being alone with the doomed animal just made both Emily and the pig nervous, like an awkward first date with a homicidal conclusion. And, they say adrenaline isn't good for the meat.

Emily, who is my wife's cousin, lives in Homer, Alaska. I'm from Anchorage. I've been coming to Homer every summer since I was a kid, and I've never lost a visitor's appreciation for it. To get a sense of the natural setting, picture every postcard you've seen from Alaska. Eagles swooping over a sparkling ocean. Glaciers cascading down snow-capped mountains. Otters cracking oyster shells. In Homer, you see all that on a five-minute walk. Sometimes I get so scenically saturated I think my eyes can't absorb one more wild, gorgeous detail. And then the sun goes down, a full moon rises over the water, and the air turns herbal with spruce sap and pushki (Alaskan cow parsnip).

People don't end up in Homer the way they might end up in Cleveland or Minneapolis or even Anchorage. There isn't one big economic draw. My mother, who has lived most of her life in Anchorage, says Homer is a place

Emily Garrity cuts herbs in preparation for the farm-to-table dinner event.

people go to manifest dreams. It sounds New Agey, but she's right. There was a time when all of Alaska was like that; I'm sure my grandparents felt that call when they drove their Buick up here from Illinois fifty years ago. Some of the state's frontier glow may have faded since then, but in Homer, it's still present. I can't think of a Homer person I know who is not right at this moment industriously creating: pottery, books. peony farms. And so many dreams in the community seem to revolve around food: In this town of five thousand there's a brewery, three from-scratch bakeries, two coffee roasting companies, a robust fishing industry, oyster farms, a lush farmers' market, and a dozen restaurants, many of their menus seasonal and local.

Emily is thirty-six, and she's a farmer. She learned how to butcher pigs the same way she's learned most everything she knows about farming: trial, error, and Google. She didn't grow up with agriculture—or guns, for that matter. The daughter of a union laborer and a community relations worker, she has a degree in photojournalism. She didn't become interested in growing things until her late teens, when she worked in a commercial greenhouse, farming basil.

She came to Homer more than a decade ago with an idea to buy some land and have a big garden. Now she has a really big garden, ten acres of farm that she calls Twitter Creek Gardens. It's named for a nearby stream, which itself was named well before the social network launched. She works the land full time; she built her own farmhouse and greenhouse. She added pigs, bees, egg chickens, and meat chickens to an acre of orderly vegetable rows—all of it carved by her own hands out of forest and wildflower fields.

Emily also got a US Department of Agriculture grant to build a high-tunnel greenhouse, a semipermanent tent-like structure, made of tall half-circle steel ribs clothed in clear polyvinyl. This shelter increased the soil temperature and extended her growing season, boosting her output. Danny Consenstein, director of the Alaska Farm Service Agency (and, in true Alaska style, also a bluegrass musician) told me he suspects that Homer now has more USDA-funded high tunnels than any other zip code in the country. They have totally revolutionized farming there, boosted the restaurant culture, and extended the availability of local produce, he said.

Emily's farm requires an astronomical amount of work. Whenever I used to slosh down the pitted road to her place, I'd reflect on the chicken filth, the endless weeding, the rain and frost, and the ever-present mud. I couldn't figure out why she did it. But I get it now. In a world of searchers, she has found her thing. A dream, manifested.

Homer has a great affinity for the culture and cuisine of Louisiana. Last month my family and I were heading down from Anchorage for Emily's boucherie—a big, weekend-long pig-butchering party very loosely modeled after community-wide parties held in the Southern state, at which people dispatch a pig together and cook up the whole thing. As my wife and I hustled our two boys out of the car, a fog had settled over the vegetable field, and I could feel winter in the September air. We were late to the slaughter: By the time we arrived, the 330-pound hog called Juvenile Delinquent, Joovy for short, was already deceased, subject to Emily's revised pig-killing protocol.

Pig meets pistol according to size, Emily explained, and size is influenced by personality. Alpha pigs, the pushier ones, get fatter quicker. Joovy was the second-pushiest in the pen, after Big Bertha, who Emily had already slaughtered and sold earlier that year. Two more hogs, Lil Red and Lucy Patch, were still happily snorting around in the mud past the field.

Of all Emily's pigs, Joovy was the only male, and she liked him best. He got his name because he was curious, always biting her tools and knocking over the water bucket. He had a thing for head rubs. "I liked his spunk," she said. "I would have kept him forever if I thought I could handle a year-round seven-hundred-pound hog."

She told me that before she shot him in the pen, she'd given a little speech about him to the assembled people who came to help. She'd carried a pistol out to the middle of the pig yard as a friend filled the trough with sprouted grain and a little molasses. All the pigs came running and buried their faces in the mush. She moved in.

"I set my intentions really sturdy first," she told me later of her process. "I say a little prayer, and then I shoot it in the head and thank it for what it is doing." The emotional constitutions of the other pigs remain intact, she explained. In fact, they don't even flinch. "They just go right back to the food trough," said Emily. "And they're like, 'Sweet. We get more food now.'"

There are more than a half-dozen micro-farming operations around Homer, including Emily's. They're serious business. Emily was at the point that the farm was just about supporting her all year-round, though she still had to pick up a little extra work substitute teaching in the wintertime. Farm tourism that included events like the boucherie was exactly the sort of thing she wanted to add to her lineup to make everything pencil out. This dinner, a test run, was mainly for friends and family. All forty of us were paying guests.

Emily dedicated the event to her Uncle Ray, a longtime Homer character who had been killed the summer before in an ATV accident while working at a remote cabin. Somewhere along the line, we'd stopped calling the weekend the boucherie, and started calling it the Bouche-Ray. Ray was a mustachioed wearer of wide-brimmed hats who liked to smoke cigars. He worked as a carpenter, but really he was a musician. He played in a Cajun band and had a way with just about every instrument. Accordion was always my favorite to hear him play.

As far as I can tell, Homer's love for Louisiana started with Uncle Ray and his partner, Jen King, who we call Aunt Fancy. They had a Cajun band for twenty-plus years called Ray-Jen Cajun. Their good friends Karen Berger and Steve McCasland, who own Homer Brewing, are from Texas originally, but Steve's grandparents live in northern Louisiana. Karen and Steve began throwing Mardi Gras parties, which over the years grew to the point of public coronation of "royalty" and a parade through town.

Eventually Karen, Steve, Ray, Jen, and a big group of bluegrass musicians from Homer and Juneau—all raging Louisianaphiles—traveled down to Cajun country proper for the Festivals Acadiens et Créoles. "By God, everybody and their mama went to Lafayette," Karen told me.

That was maybe eight years ago. More trips were made after that. More parades put on. More paper bag–brown roux mixed around in Steve's gumbo pot. It was Ray who first suggested Emily raise a pig or two. When he died, we marched down Homer's short main street in a New Orleans–style second-line parade, waving hankies, beating tambourines, weeping, and marching in the saints with saxes and tubas. Homer has this kind of magic to it. It's the culture to dream things up and wholeheartedly take part.

A hog feeds at Twitter Creek Gardens, near Homer.

Hog fat is rendered over a wood fire at Twitter Creek Gardens.

A long table dominated Emily's small living room and a roll of butcher paper hung from the ceiling. When we walked in, she was at the stove, where a pot bubbled away, giving off aromas of wine and sage. I had been with my wife, Sara, for fourteen years, and known Emily long enough that I don't remember when we met. She played music at our big Anchorage wedding in 2008. When our second son was born in June, I texted her a picture from the delivery room.

Sara and I both come from enormous Irish-Italian families. Her mother has nine siblings, my father has eight. The aunts, uncles, and cousins go on for miles, an extended network crisscrossing Alaska. As I fell for Sara, I fell in with her family and friends. Her sister and brother-in-law played in a bluegrass band in Juneau. Sara's people were different from the law school–bound city girls I'd been trying to understand in college. Nobody stressed about work. They weren't preoccupied with titles or degrees. They worked to live, and by live, I mean play music, make art, fish, cook, and drink really good beer. There's something to be said for being present in your life, for appreciating what is. I can lose track of that, living in the city and facing the relentless time problem that is working and having children, but being on Emily's farm reminds me.

Two guys hunched over Emily's table, wiping sweat on their T-shirts, sawing hunks of flesh off long bones. I recognized a belly slab as bacon. The pig's head, feet, and organs were neatly arranged in a hotel pan. A saw, a mallet, and some sticky-looking knives were strewn about among open butchering books. I stepped on a wayward chunk of raw pig fat with my bare foot.

After Emily shoots a pig, she told me, she slits its throat and bleeds it right away, before "death throes" set in. (Death throes are when the three-hundred-pound pig starts thrashing around, spasming even after death.) Then she throws the animal on its back, dehairs it, guts it, and quarters it. In the last five years, Emily had slaughtered and butchered eleven pigs. Back when she did the first one, she and a couple of friends cut up the carcass according to how one of them remembered dressing deer. What they ended up with was a bit of a mess, "a lot of sausage and a couple roasts," she recalled. Now, on her twelfth pig, all the cuts—picnic roasts, Boston butt, ham hocks, bacon—were being mapped out according to the books. The pieces were separated, wrapped, and labeled.

When I arrived, Emily and her team had been at work breaking down the pig for thirty-six hours, with short breaks for sleeping. Every six hours or so, Emily prepared a pork dish so everyone could refuel. I stopped to admire two thick loins just before they splashed into a bucket of brine. "I don't feel tired. I'm so excited. Being tired doesn't even register," Emily said.

Homer's food scene has matured significantly in the past five years. Much of this is because demand has grown: Locals like good food, and increasingly the town is a destination for seasonal residents from Anchorage and Outside who have money to spend at restaurants and markets. Every time I visit, a new restaurant has opened, and there are more vacation houses built where once there was empty land.

To get to Homer, you simply drive south from Anchorage until the highway ends five hours later. It is, literally, the end of the road. The town rambles down a lush hillside to the rocky shore of Kachemak Bay; its most distinctive feature is a narrow peninsula known as the Spit that juts out about four and a half miles into the water. A road runs down the spine of the Spit, with businesses and beaches along either side. The harbor is located toward the end, near a literal-minded hotel called Land's End.

Kachemak Bay and the surrounding land are rich in seafood, edible plants, and game, and the area was traveled by Alaska Natives for thousands of years before European and Russian explorers landed there in the late 1700s. Homer began as a small coal-mining—and then a short-lived gold-mining—operation in the 1890s, and slowly grew. Much of the area was settled by homesteaders. What is now downtown Homer is land that, around 1920, belonged to just one dairy farm.

Today, if you were to walk down the aisles of one of Homer's two grocery stores, you'd probably pass a married couple or two from the neighboring Russian Old Believer religious communities. The young women would be wearing headscarves that matched their floor-length skirts, and they'd likely be pushing babies in their carts. You'd also probably see an unshowered fisherman in a gut-splattered hoodie and Xtratuf boots. There would be somebody with dreadlocks, and also maybe a retired judge from Anchorage who has a second home in town.

The chef for the big dinner was a thin, serious-looking guy named Brian Grobleski. He'd trained at the Culinary Institute of America and worked in restaurants in a number of cities, including a recent stint in Chicago, where he'd been at a place called Floriole. He opened the fridge, and I peered in at Joovy's head on the shelf above the produce drawer.

Brian came to Homer in 2012 through the World Wide Opportunities on Organic Farms program, sort of a Couchsurfing.org for people with an interest in organic farming, and landed a job on a farm run by the Kilcher family. (This was just about the time the family, relations of the pop singer Jewel, became the subject of the reality television show "Alaska: The Last Frontier." Reality television is epidemic here. Everybody you meet in every small town is either on it, working for it, or one degree away from it.)

He swirled a jar of nasturtium vinaigrette and offered me some to taste. It was bright with a radishy heat. He told me that he'd come to Homer in

Chefs Brian Grobleski and Preston Jones prepare food for a five-course farm-to-table dinner held in one of Twitter Creek Gardens' greenhouses.

search of a new relationship with ingredients: "When you go to other cities, it seems like there's such an attempt to manipulate the food rather than appreciate what's already there." He was tired of kitchens driven by competition, where preparations seemed to grow increasingly complex. The very food itself seemed anxious to him, and he needed to get away. "I had my chapter in life of turning things into foams and jellies," he said. "To me, it wasn't genuine." He wanted to work on a farm directly.

Brian's not alone in his move—or his motivations. I've met so many former food service folks who came to Homer and became farm people that I came up with a term for them: chefugees. Brian and Emily met at the

FOLLOWING: As the sun sets in the early fall, festive lights glow and plates are warmed over a fire outside the dining greenhouse at Twitter Creek Gardens.

farmers' market where they sold vegetables at adjacent booths. Meeting Emily reinvigorated his love for cooking, he said. She works so hard that others can't help but work hard too.

Homer has an intimate sense of culinary ecosystem. Farmers know chefs. Chefs know diners. Homer residents are sophisticated eaters, making a strong support network for culinary businesses. Kirsten Dixon, a chef and cookbook author, co-owns La Baleine, a summer-only restaurant on the Homer Spit, and also runs the nearby Tutka Bay Lodge, where she offers cooking classes on an old crab boat. "I love it when the crusty old guy is an expert on Italian wines, or the fisherman who walks in has a passion for mushrooms," she said to me. "We really have a vibrant culture and food scene."

Cooking is identity; it brings connection to place. Alaska gets this totally; Homer might get it most of all. To be sure, there are good restaurant meals to be had in the state, but not many outside a few of the larger towns. Once you head out on the highway in any direction, it's nothing but Crunchwrap Supremes, gas station Slim Jims, diner eggs, and sugary white chocolate mochas. The wintertime produce and the prevalence of Anywhere-America strip-mall food breed in Alaskans a sense of deprivation. This is what spurs Alaskans to carry Bubble Wrap in their suitcases when they go on vacation so they can return home with bottles of Harissa sauce, jars of Trader Joe's Cookie Butter, and French cheeses available at reasonable prices. I'm certain it is part of the reason so many people in Alaska are good cooks.

Here, self-sustenance—what Alaska Natives call "subsistence"—is at the heart of eating: fishing, hunting, gathering, and canning. Alaskans forage. We pick berries, hunt mushrooms, and gather seaweed. Because of the long winters, food preservation is a common fall activity. Certain fish smoking techniques are closely guarded family secrets. In some circles, pickles function as currency. Salted salmon roe is a delicacy, and sourdough starter an heirloom.

Our plates most often center on seafood. Salmon is widely available, affordable, and spectacular. Other fish, moose, caribou, and birds are common meals too. The stars of the cultivated produce world are root vegetables and crucifers like broccoli, cauliflower, and cabbage. No matter where

Guests socialize in the greenhouse during the dinner.

in the world you are, cooking is identity; it brings connection to place. Alaska gets this totally; Homer might get it most of all.

By dinnertime the next day, Emily's farm was transformed. The butchering crew had finished with Joovy and joined a larger dinner crew, who turned their attention to the grounds. Emily's sister Julia screen printed napkins and aprons. Others flattened out the big greenhouse floor and built a plywood stage. Two long tables were constructed from plywood. Christmas lights were strung from the greenhouse ceiling. Out-of-town guests began to arrive. Some of them planned to spend the night, and they pitched tents in the yard. A bossa nova band set up. Voices and music filled the greenhouse.

The meal was, naturally, spectacular. The salad with nasturtium dressing was served with a scoop of homemade ricotta and sweet Chiogga beets shaved so thin that light shone through them. There was an earthy carrot soup, a warm salad of patty-pan squash and root vegetables, and that pork loin, bathed in a maple gastrique. Dessert was chamomile panna cotta and tiny scones made with pork fat. The sunset glowed pink through the corrugated plastic roof, and then a supermoon rose.

The next day, the crew was back in butchering mode, gathered around a big extruder in the yard, pumping fat casings full of sausage. A big outdoor burner kept a long-simmering pot of gumbo warm. We'd lost some of our number from the night before, but there were thirty or so of us still on the farm. We watched the chickens mill in the yard, stoked the fire, and ate fresh-picked greens by the handful out of a big basket.

Emily set about making pig-head posole in an outdoor kitchen. Aunt Fancy and a couple members of Uncle Ray's old Cajun band played in the greenhouse. The accordion lilted clear and sad. I two-stepped the baby on the dirt floor. Earlier in the day, a chicken had been killed, plucked, and butchered. Robbi Mixon pulled it from a buttermilk bath, floured it, and fried it up in a pot of bubbling fresh lard.

Robbi is thirty-three; she runs the Homer farmers' market. She's a semi-recent Homer transplant, having moved from San Francisco, where she worked as an event planner. Homer had grown on her, she told me. She likes running into people she knows in the grocery store. She'd been vegetarian for years, and then she fell in with Emily, and Emily's pigs. "I really connected to my food source," Robbi said. "So eating meat felt better."

A bunch of us stood around the pot waiting for pieces of the bird, our breath making clouds in the night air. In perhaps the best moment of the weekend, I watched my picky three-year-old take his first-ever bite of fried chicken, perfectly crisp and salty. His pants were slick with mud and his hands were filthy. "I like this," he said.

Sunday morning, we all needed Advil with our coffee. Most people rolled up their tents and hit the road, and I offered to cook dinner later for the few of us who remained. Something simple, I said. Something low-key.

I decided on pasta, hot and garlicky, with the pork sausage that had been cased the previous day. As the dinner hour approached, more guests began to arrive. This was Homer, so everyone had an offering: thin rounds of spicy, pickled squash; tofu dip; fresh peas; fresh collards; a container of homemade red sauce; a hunk of Danish blue cheese; a bottle of Prosecco; a growler of Homer Brewing Company Bitter. I started out expecting six at the table, but my phone kept buzzing with additions. Soon we were twelve. Then sixteen.

"Is it all right?" our friends would ask, before heading over.

"Sure, sure," I replied. "We have plenty of room at the table."

Carri Thurman and Sharon Roufa
BAKERS AT THE FRONT OF AN AGRICULTURAL REVOLUTION

Carri Thurman and Sharon Roufa run Two Sisters Bakery in Homer, a landmark restaurant and bakery that began in 1993. Over time, they have watched as Homer has been transformed by a boom in small farms, often known as "gardens" or "micro-farms," which have in turn helped to support a crop of innovative, seasonal restaurants, transforming the small coastal community in Southcentral Alaska into a culinary hub. The local farms have grown with the help of government grants to build greenhouses that have extended the growing season. Climate change has also brought warmer temperatures that have encouraged farmers to try growing more and different foods. Thurman and Roufa describe how Alaskan diners in Homer tend also to be well-traveled with sophisticated tastes. Many are also competent home cooks, very capable at wild food processing and preparation, with high expectations for what appears on restaurant plates.

Julia: Can you tell me from what vantage point you view Alaska's food culture?

Carri: We're on the front line of the food battle, no joke, you know. Like when the power goes out, you would think that people would go home. But they come to the bakery. It's one of those places that you know. We hear from people all the time saying, "We've been planning our trip around getting a sticky bun at Two Sisters," or, planning my day around getting these things here, and really communicating with people about what they like and what they need. Sharon was a huge part of the opening of the farmers' market years ago. She was one of the founding members and that to me was a really huge moment for Homer. It had been talked about for so many years. To finally make it happen and look at it now, you know the availability of things. Our ability to talk to these farmers and say, "If you grow it, we'll cook it," you know? I do kind of draw the line at kohlrabi but everything else I'm totally OK with.

Julia: Have you seen the impact of climate change in terms of sourcing, cooking, and in what way?

Carri: Apples. We get cases of apples at the end of summer in the past five years that we never did before. We're getting produce now that we just weren't getting before.

Sharon: We also had our first paralytic shellfish poisoning scare that impacted local oyster farms, and locals who gather clams and mussels. [Alaska has had more recent PSP outbreaks, which have been linked to warmer ocean temperatures.]

Carri: Yes, that's true. Apples and asparagus—those are the two things we're getting now that we never did locally before. Like Alaskan asparagus. People were like, "What?!" You know what I mean. Granted, they're grown in a high tunnel but still.

Julia: And the influence of high tunnels?

Sharon: Oh that's huge, especially for the farmers' market. When we first started there wasn't much of anything. We started the farmers' market in the middle of summer and went from there. And then the first full year it started on the summer solstice. Now with common use of the high tunnels, the farmers' market starts at the end of May and there's already produce available. So it's almost a whole month earlier that we're able to get produce, and the growing season goes later into the fall, too.

Carri: We have a woman who brings us fresh herbs almost year-round. She has a little lull in January and February, but we're getting nasturtium blossoms in February and March from this local person, from her high tunnel.

Julia: We're familiar with California cuisine or Southern cuisine. What would you say Alaska's cuisine is?

Carri: I think it really starts with the land and the sea and how we make do with what we have from here. I think the root is in subsistence and what we can gather and how we make the best use of that. You know to call it a cuisine, it's hard to pin that down. I feel like it's a melting pot depending on whose food you're eating and where they came from.

Sharon: I'd say Alaska cuisine is "making do." It's the cuisine of making do.

Carri: [laughs] That's a really good point.

Sharon: As a restaurant when you're trying to produce food for locals, you are hosting people who already know how to can bear or how to dress up a salmon or who have a freezer full of halibut. And you need to take it one more step. People here have been making do and doing their own thing to save money. There's not a store you can always run out to. Maybe you live thirty minutes out of town anyway, or you don't want to have to get the kids in their snowsuits just to get one more thing. And you're not just running to your neighbor to get a cup of sugar. You're like, what can I use instead of sugar? How can I do this? And if you've ever been to a potluck in Homer, it's outstanding. There's amazing dishes people have created that I get inspired by all the time.

Carri: Yes, everybody's got their jam. Literally.

Sharon: We've got our job cut out for us. It's not like trying to serve somebody in New York where they don't even know how to cook. It's a little harder to impress. The game plan is just a lot more of making do and of doing it yourself—kind of a big DIY situation.

Carri: We really enjoy running our kitchen that way, too, you know. That's how the sweet potatoes focaccia sandwiches came about. People love them. We've been doing those now for fifteen years, and because it's the middle of winter and there are no other vegetables available to put on anything, they seem more interesting. We sliced up a sweet potato and roasted it and put it on a turkey sandwich and everybody just went, "Whaaaaat?!"

It's like literally our whole business is built that way in a lot of respects.

EASY ALLEY RASPBERRY JAM

AT LEAST 2 (8-OUNCE) JARS

I've been working this week on the easiest possible raspberry jam recipe and, to fuel my experiments, I've been picking raspberries from a bush that grows from a neighbor's yard over the fence into my alley for a couple summers. The house recently sold, but before that, it was occupied by the same woman for probably fifty years until she died. The raspberry patch is a common Alaska kind: a thick and spidery tangle, heavy with fruit, creeping into the yards around it. Anchorage's older neighborhoods have alleys and those alleys have raspberries. My dad, who grew up in such a neighborhood in downtown Anchorage, told me it was very practical to have a raspberry bush when he was growing up. The bushes grow well in Alaska's climate, are hugely prolific, and make fruit that can be frozen and jammed. Delicate berries didn't used to be able to survive the trip up north, he told me. Even now, a handful-sized carton out of season can cost as much as six dollars.

My kids aren't big on jam (they are peanut-butter-obsessed weirdos), but I had to make three batches to get it right. One evening during my jam testing period, I left for a walk. At the time, I had a whole bunch of jewel-tone jars on my counter and a question in my head: What will I do with this jam?

A few hours later, on my way back from the walk, I saw a woman slipping out of the fence in the yard of the house with the raspberries. The house wasn't occupied, so I asked her who she was. Her eyes welled. She was the niece of the old woman who used to live in the house, she said. Her father, the old woman's brother, was out of state, dying, she said. She wasn't sure he'd make it through the night. She couldn't be with her family, she said, but she "just had to pick some raspberries" to feel connected to them.

And then I knew what to do with my jam. I went home and got her a jar.

3½ to 4 cups raspberries
1¾ to 2 cups sugar
Juice of ½ lemon

This jam recipe requires no pectin and is pretty hard to mess up. If you want, you can sterilize the jars before you fill them and process them for 5

minutes in boiling water (following the canning jar instructions to "can" the jam).

Wash jars with hot soap and water. (I like to put them in the dishwasher and pull them out to fill when they are still hot.)

In a large pot over medium heat and using a wooden spoon, add the raspberries, sugar, and lemon juice, and stir to combine well, mashing some of the berries. Bring the mixture to a boil, stirring constantly, then turn down the heat to low, stirring and scraping down the sides of the pan for about 30 minutes, until the jam has a thicker, syrupy consistency.

Pour the jam into the clean jars. The jam will thicken as it cools. Screw the jar lids on. Store the jam in an airtight jar in the refrigerator for up to two weeks or in the freezer for up to 3 months. (For the jam to go in the freezer, leave a ¼-inch headroom between the jam and the lid for freezer expansion.) Give a jar to a friend.

Chapter 10

Thousands of Miles from Washington, DC, the Gwich'in Track the Fate of Caribou Country

To understand the relationship between the indigenous Gwich'in Athabas-cans, who live in Arctic Village near the edge of the Arctic National Wildlife Refuge (ANWR) and the massive caribou herd that migrates through their land twice yearly, you might start in February with a ride on the back of Charlie Swaney's old snowmobile. You will motor past his sled-dog yard and head along a trail that leads out of the village through the powdery snow. After fifteen minutes, you'll reach a wide frozen lake, and he'll slow down so as not to scare the animals. There might have been fifty caribou along the distant shoreline on a recent afternoon. In late winter they dig through the snow with their shovel-shaped hooves, looking for lichen, their food.

Swaney silences the engine, gets off, swings the rifle off his back, and examines the line of animal shapes through his scope. *Pop!* The herd scatters, leaving one female down. Soon Swaney is kneeling next to it with his knife. The head comes off first. Then the skin, beginning with a gentle slit down the white belly. The Gwich'in have been hunting caribou in this region for thousands of years.

Charlie Swaney heads out at dawn to hunt caribou.

Groceries are delivered by small plane to Arctic Village, considered one of the most remote communities in the country.

"You got to respect the animal, because that's how you eat," Swaney says, as he pulls hide from muscle. "You don't take too many," he says. "What you don't eat, you feed to the dogs.

Respect is the main thing."

In twenty minutes, the caribou is butchered and on the sled, and Swaney is kicking snow over its entrails. He's so expert at the process, he can do it blind. Swaney, fifty-four, was an orphan, taught to hunt by his grandparents, who raised him. His most important job in the village is one for which he isn't paid. He's a provider of meat. People in the village are of modest means, but they are rich in caribou. And that is what keeps the village alive, he says. "The lifestyle out here is different," Swaney says, raising his chin toward the caribou. "That's why we depend on what's out there."

Since the late 1980s, the Gwich'in people, who live in fifteen villages that stretch from Alaska into Canada, have been deeply involved in a fight to stop the push for oil development on the coastal plain of the Arctic National Wildlife Refuge. Alaska is home to several massive herds of caribou. One of the largest, known as the Porcupine Caribou Herd, more than 219,000 animals, migrates annually through Gwich'in land in the spring as it heads to the arctic coast to calve, returning just as the snow starts to fly.

Although the Gwich'in have been championed by environmental groups, they say they are not environmentalists but are instead human rights advocates. The health of the caribou is their central concern because village economies depend on it, says Sarah James, an Arctic Village elder who is often tapped to speak to the media. Oil drilling will impact the herd's behavior, she says. "We have seen oil spills, big spills, or even small spills. There is no way of cleaning up the coastal plain, which is tundra. It is too risky."

Drilling had not yet been permitted in the refuge in 2015, despite heavy lobbying over many years. In January, the Obama administration had proposed designating just over twelve million additional acres of the refuge as wilderness, a change that would have created further barriers to oil development. The designation change required an act of Congress and was unsuccessful. Nevertheless, environmental groups cheered the proposal, and Alaska politicians from Juneau to Washington reacted angrily, calling a number of press conferences. Alaska's state government is funded primarily by oil revenue. The state is currently facing a budget crisis linked to the low price of oil.

Alaska US Senator Dan Sullivan called the announcement an act of war. US Senator Lisa Murkowski said it was a "gut punch," and later threatened to crimp the Department of the Interior's budget in response. US Representative Don Young's office said it was like spitting in the faces of Alaskans. In Juneau, legislators called a press conference and made floor speeches excoriating the federal government.

In Arctic Village, 230 miles north of Fairbanks, just across the East Fork of the Chandalar River from the refuge, Gwich'in people watched stories about ANWR on TV news delivered to their living rooms by satellite. They saw on the Internet that most every national outlet covered Obama's announcement. Stories quoted politicians, environmental groups, and oil company

Sarah James, a longtime Gwich'in activist who opposes the opening of ANWR to drilling

spokespeople, but few mentioned their point of view. A few Gwich'in leaders wrote editorials published in Alaska papers, but that was all the world heard from them. "It was as if we did not exist," James says. "But we have been here for thousands of years."

Still, villagers are very happy about a proposed wilderness designation. "I can't stop smiling, that's how good the news is to me," Sarah James says. They hope the president will go further, circumventing Congress and using his power to designate the land as a national monument. Among all the parties with a stake in whether drilling happens in ANWR, they feel they have the most to lose, she says.

"We support one hundred percent keeping it closed," says Ernie Peter, an Arctic Village tribal council member and former chief. "It is for our younger generation."

Should the caribou be harmed and their numbers reduced, people wouldn't have the food they depend on and would likely have to move,

James says. Village life sustains a fragile culture. There are only eight thousand Gwich'in total in Alaska and Canada, James says. In Alaska, there are now fewer than three hundred people fluent in Gwich'in.

The Porcupine Herd is very healthy. There are more animals in the herd now than there has ever been since scientists started to study it in the 1980s, according to Jason Caikoski, assistant area biologist for Northeast Alaska with the state Department of Fish and Game. For two decades, they calved in a part of the refuge at the center of the drilling dispute, a stretch of coastal land where scientists determined billions of barrels of oil may lie belowground. Recently, however, the majority of them have moved east into Canada to calve, Caikoski says. "Why they have shifted calving, we don't know. Whether they will return [to their traditional calving grounds], we don't know."

One of the larger questions in the debate is whether drilling operations, if they were to intersect with calving caribou in ANWR, would have a negative effect. The Central Arctic Herd that calves near northern Prudhoe Bay oil-drilling operations has only increased in number, Caikoski says, since drilling began. This fact is often cited by drilling proponents. On the other hand, he says, studies have shown that caribou avoid disturbances, which could include equipment related to oil drilling. "Whether that has a population effect, that's the big question," he says, adding that scientists don't have enough data to predict what will happen.

Gwich'in elders tell stories about periods of starvation, when caribou numbers plummeted for unknown reasons. Even in those times, they say, hunters never disturbed calving animals. Even if other caribou coexist with drilling apparatus elsewhere, their herd is sensitive.

"Sure there's a lot now, but we know from experience, we always have to be careful because that can crash," says Kay Wallis, a board member of the Gwich'in Steering Committee, the organization that represents the Gwich'in.

When Swaney returns from hunting, he finds his wife, Marion, and her sister, Martha, at a cardboard-covered table with knives and a hacksaw,

FOLLOWING: Caribou from the Porcupine Herd milling just outside of town on a frozen lake

dividing up a caribou he'd shot the day before. They parcel it into old bread bags to be frozen. The rest of the carcass is spread out on the floor. CNN blares on the television. A cat, one of two in the village, winds itself around the table legs.

Swaney built the cabin himself. In the kitchen, the food shelves hold packages of pasta, dried mashed potatoes, rice, Folgers coffee, Crisco. Because propane has become so expensive, their family, like most people in the village, shuns using a stove and instead cooks with a hot plate and a microwave. Electricity costs them 100 dollars a month. Marion has a job at the school, working in the cafeteria.

Average household income in the village is 27,000 dollars, and the cost of living is high. The clinic, school, and tribe provide some work. Lots of people work several small jobs. Children make up about a third of the population. Groceries at the local store are three times what they cost in Fairbanks. A bag of Doritos might be ten dollars, a can of Folgers, sixteen dollars. Gas for snow machines—which is what Alaskans call snowmobiles—costs ten dollars a gallon, and it takes fifty dollars to fill the tank. There is only one working truck in Arctic Village.

This is also a corner of America where there is still no indoor plumbing. Villagers haul water. The call of nature is answered with a five-gallon plastic "honey bucket" with a toilet seat on top. The village of 150 has one working public shower, which costs users five dollars each.

Locals stay busy with the chores of everyday life. Aside from hunting and fishing, everyone heats with wood, which must be hauled from the hillside by snow machine and chopped. Sometimes people might not have cash for gas or even electricity, but they always have food, Swaney says. "You're never stingy with it. You got someone needs meat, you give it to them; it'll come back to you."

Arctic Village and the neighboring village of Venetie are not like most Alaska Native communities. Alaska does not have a reservation system like the Lower 48 states. Most Alaska Natives are shareholders in regional corporations, which manage land and invest money, paying dividends. When the corporations were formed, Arctic Village and Venetie chose not to participate, winning instead the title to nearly two million acres of land. To come into the village, outsiders need permission from the tribal council. To explore the land outside the village, they must be accompanied by a Gwich'in guide.

Outsiders must request permission from the tribal council to come into the village.

Other segments of the Alaska Native community support drilling in ANWR, especially in the North Slope Borough, which has benefited from development in the oil fields at Prudhoe Bay. Many Native corporations are invested in oil. The Gwich'in in Alaska looked into drilling on their land in the early 1980s, but elders soon felt the exploration was too big of a disturbance, Sarah James says. In 1988, elders from all the Gwich'in villages came together to discuss whether they would support oil development in ANWR's coastal plain, and decided against it. There were too many unknowns when it came to the animals, they decided.

Elders then designated people to advocate for that position. Sarah James was among those chosen. Her assignment, she was told, would last until her death. She is now seventy-one years old. A long white ponytail hangs down her back. She is one of just a few people who remember the village when everyone spoke Gwich'in except the Episcopal missionaries. "My term was for life, because this is our life," she says. "That's what the elders tell us."

Charlie Swaney butchers a caribou outside of the village.

Sarah James's brother Gideon, seventy-six, a former tribal chief, lives in a family cabin, with walls decorated with Christmas wrapping paper, caribou antler carvings, and family photographs. He's a news junkie, who tracked every development since the president's announcement. When a visitor asks him his opinion, he rises from his couch and opens a notebook where he writes down things he hears people say on the news that he wants to refute. "I can hear what our senators, our politicians, are saying but there is no way for me to go confront them," he says.

Contacted for this story, Senator Sullivan declined to comment. Young, who is from the Gwich'in community of Fort Yukon, declined as well. Senator Lisa Murkowski's office sent a statement from a staffer, saying the senator had introduced legislation that would require oil companies to "meet the highest level of environmental protection and mitigation available." The healthy caribou herd at Prudhoe Bay is proof of that, the statement says. "Alaska has a proven track record of prudent development and environmentally responsible oil and gas production."

Gideon James says he remembers when oil was first discovered in Prudhoe Bay. Things didn't turn out the way politicians said, he says. "There was this big push, excitement," he remembers. "There was a promise of better living conditions, better education, better health service. Where are they?" Oil companies made a killing, he says, but the state didn't take a big enough share. Now Alaska is facing a budget crisis. "It's a shame to be that broke, with so many resources the state has," he says.

Politicians don't take into account how fragile life is in the village, he explains. They don't respect the traditional migration routes of the animals, the caribou and birds who pass through Gwich'in land on the way north. James wishes Alaska's politicians would visit to get a sense of the Gwich'in life.

Down the road, in the tribal hall, Peter, the former chief, says the same thing. The president also has a standing invitation, he says. "I heard he's coming to Alaska," he says. "So maybe he'll make it up this way."

POSTSCRIPT: In late 2017, with the support of the Trump administration, Congress passed legislation allowing for leasing and oil exploration in ANWR.

MAKES 10 SERVINGS

It's the end of moose season, the wind's howling as I write this, and we're all settling into our winter routines. Doesn't chili sound good? This recipe isn't just any chili; it's chili with a story, a little culinary snapshot of a moment in time in Alaska's history. And, with a couple of tweaks, it's very good.

As far as I can tell, Alaska Governor Sarah Palin's chili recipe was introduced to the nation in 2013. It was published in her Christmas book, discussed by Fox TV News, and showed up on at least one reality TV show. But Palin started feeding local reporters her slow-cooker chili way before 2013, even before she ran for vice president in 2008. A number of my Alaska journalism colleagues have crumbled corn chips into steamy bowls of chili in her kitchen. "I remember thinking it would be rude not to try it," said Kyle Hopkins, who covered politics at the *Anchorage Daily News* back then.

Sure, the chili became a public-relations dish with a folksy message about the candidate and the place she comes from. But maybe for a moment, way back when she was regularly talking with Alaska reporters in her Wasilla kitchen, it had something to say about our Alaska and how we cook that's actually true.

I spent a week with the recipe, and with a bit of tricking out, it's great. Beyond that, it's super practical and uses pantry and freezer stores, which is truly Alaskan.

Here's the thing: A can of kidney beans currently costs ninety-nine cents at Walmart. So you can make Sarah Palin's chili, which serves eight to ten people, for less than ten dollars, if you've already got ground moose meat in the freezer. And those canned

2 pounds ground meat (moose, caribou, beef, bison, musk ox, or a combination)
1 large white onion
1 tablespoon vegetable oil (if needed)
4 (15-ounce) cans pinto beans, drained and rinsed
4 (15-ounce) cans kidney beans, drained and rinsed
2 (15-ounce) cans tomato sauce
1 (10-ounce) can Ro-Tel diced tomatoes and green chiles, and the juices
1 (12-ounce) can dark beer
2 (1-ounce) packets taco seasoning (or make your own; see following recipe)
Optional toppings: grated Cheddar cheese, sour cream, chopped green onions, hot taco sauce, corn chips

beans just hang out in your pantry until you're in a pinch and need to feed a crowd. The recipe only requires maybe ten minutes of prep and can sit on the counter in the slow cooker for half a day. What working mother in America can't get behind something like that on, say, a Wednesday night before basketball practice?

Palin's recipe had four ingredients: 8 cans kidney beans, 1 pound ground moose meat, 2 cans tomato sauce, and 2 packages taco seasoning, 1 regular and 1 hot. My recipe stays with the easy, Alaska shelf-stable freezer bounty vibe, but I use homemade taco seasoning and add a can of beer (I use a can of Alaska-brewed porter, but a Bud Light works too).

Sauté the meat in a large skillet over medium-high heat until browned, 7 to 10 minutes, stirring frequently with a wooden spoon. Spoon most of the fat out of the pan and discard. Put the meat into the crock of a slow cooker.

Finely chop the onion. Add the onion to the fat in the skillet and sauté over medium heat until soft, about 5 minutes. (If you are using all wild game meat, which can be very lean, you may need to add 1 tablespoon vegetable oil for sautéing.) Add the onion to the slow cooker.

Add the pinto beans, kidney beans, tomato sauce, Ro-Tel tomatoes and chiles, beer, and taco seasoning, and stir to combine. Put the lid on the slow cooker, and cook on high for 2 hours or on low for 4 hours.

MAKE-YOUR-OWN TACO SEASONING

ENOUGH TACO SEASONING FOR 2 POUNDS MEAT

- 2 tablespoons chili powder
- 1 tablespoon ground cumin
- 1 tablespoon paprika (smoked or sweet)
- 1 teaspoon salt
- 1 teaspoon onion powder
- 1 teaspoon garlic powder
- 2 teaspoons dried oregano
- 2 teaspoons cornstarch (optional), as thickener

In a small bowl, combine all the ingredients. Store in a small lidded glass jar in a dark cupboard for about 2 weeks.

Afterword

Doughnuts at the Edge of the World

If you fly about three hours west out of Anchorage on a Sunday afternoon, along the spine of the Aleutian Islands that separate the Gulf of Alaska from the Bering Sea, and you land in Adak, you'll walk off the plane into an otherworldly place, stunning in its misty, Middle Earth–like grassy hills, rare for its isolation from technology, and rich in military history.

Also, if you're lucky, you'll be there in time for doughnuts.

Adak, population maybe ninety, is one of the most far-flung American communities you can get to by jet. Its few residents make their homes on a large abandoned military base on the island, which was home to thousands during World War II. Much of the town is ghostly: the boarded-up elementary school, empty commissary, childless neighborhood playgrounds, and wind-battered vacant houses being slowly disassembled by nature. But the longer you spend there, the more your view changes, like your eyes getting used to the dark. Instead of seeing its emptiness, you see its hardy community.

Everything in Adak used to be something else. City Hall used to be the high school. The store, which is only open two hours a day (because after that, electricity costs eat all the profits), used to be a community center. The Navy-issue hutches holding beer and wine at the liquor store used to be in somebody's living room. The Bluebird Café (the only restaurant in town) is in a house on a suburban-feeling cul-de-sac, and the only way you know it's a restaurant is the OPEN sign out front. About half the neighboring houses are empty.

On certain Sunday nights, Imelda Cleary, who was born in the Philippines and runs the restaurant with her husband, Michael Rainey, pads around the

Imelda Cleary cuts out doughnuts to fry.

little kitchen, filling the bowl of her KitchenAid mixer with warm water, sugar, and yeast. When the yeast bubbles, she shakes in the flour.

"I don't really measure; I just do it by my eyes," she says.

By that time of night, business at the restaurant has slowed. Maybe there's a fish plant worker or two, or a contractor in town disposing of the old unexploded ordnance the military left behind. The menu is part American favorites (bacon cheeseburgers and homemade pizza) and part dishes of the Philippines (pancit bihon and lumpia).

Cleary and Rainey met when they were working in the commissary on a Navy base in Lemoore, California. They came to Adak in 2012 to work at the Icicle fish plant. Cleary was hired to work in the kitchen. The couple has five children between them.

Since the Navy base closed in the mid-1990s, the fish plant has been Adak's biggest employer. It seems always to be in a cycle of boom and bust. Owners come and go. It opens, drawing workers and filling the twice-weekly jet, and closes again, emptying out the town.

When the plant closed last time, Cleary and Rainey decided to stay. There was something they liked about Adak, with its familiar faces and the predictable rhythms of the fishing and crab seasons. Internet service is so expensive in town that most people don't have access. You'll never see anyone staring at an iPhone.

When she makes doughnuts, Cleary makes enough dough for eight batches. She lets it rise and then cuts the sweet, soft dough into rounds, filling sheet pans. Early Monday morning, as most of Adak sleeps, she melts Crisco in her big pan and begins to fry.

Once the doughnuts are cool, Cleary fills and frosts them. Glistening chocolate or maple icing, and custard on the inside. Word travels. Pretty soon, there are faces in the doorway. "It's kind of like the watering hole for the community. Everybody goes there; they know what day she's going to have the doughnuts," says Mary Nelson, who has lived in Adak since 1997. "People see each other. We visit."

As I pored over community cookbooks while researching for this book, I thought a lot about how food functioned as a way to connect us to each other when the outside world felt far away. There's *The Fairbanks Cook Book of Tested Recipes* from 1909, a church cookbook full of sweets and cakes, many of them very elegant, requiring dairy, butter, and eggs in a time of little refrigeration. Fairbanks would have been a very young boomtown then, built by the quest for gold. The women, wives transplanted from Seattle or San Francisco, would have been far from what they were used to, enduring a rough culture in darkness with subzero temperatures. The cookbook was put together by a church group, each recipe signed at the bottom, with very few recipes that used wild local ingredients. The collection struck me as a way of holding on to the cuisine of another, more "civilized" place, keeping the feelings of isolation at bay.

The doughnut, that tantalizing treat made of flour, sugar, and fat, which I found in many community cookbooks from the past one hundred years, is bound up with Alaska's food history, the story of the colonization of our

FOLLOWING: Remnants of military housing remain mostly abandoned after the closure of the naval base on Adak.

Imelda Cleary displays fresh doughnuts, one of the most popular items she serves at the Bluebird Café in Adak.

indigenous peoples and, further, of the Native communities' ability to adapt. Flour was one of the first Outside foods introduced to Alaska's Natives as missionaries and explorers traveled around the coast and down the rivers. Over time, those communities made that food their own. Doughnuts and fry bread have become a central part of the Alaska Native food tradition of the past 150 years. They are served at community celebrations in every region of the state.

I've found myself in Adak twice now, and both times, after hiking out in the rainy emptiness and staring at the wide horizon over the ocean, going to the Bluebird Café and biting into a fresh maple doughnut brought a similar comfort. That maple flavor is just the same as the maple bars I ate in the basement of Holy Family Cathedral in Anchorage after mass when I was a kid. The wind might be howling and my phone might be unable to get texts, but it comforts me and satisfies my longing for home.

I think the way we relate to food in Alaska starts with the mix of desires I had in that moment. Whether it's Alaska Natives in a village, eating wild foods in ancient preparations, urban Natives eating foods sent from the villages, pioneer recipe writers, an Anchorage sushi chef from Japan, or a group of people coming together to butcher a pig on a farm in Homer, food bridges our wide distances, connects us to each other, and binds us to our histories.

Alaska's cuisine is one part wild, one part shelf-stable, ever practical, seasonal, and inventive, marked by cultural contrasts, with ingredients ranging from seaweed to sheet cake to pancit to Tang. As chefs globally trend back to the local and the wild, the future of Alaska's food will continue to respond to culture, climate, and creativity.

VILLAGE-STYLE DOUGHNUTS (SUNSHINE DOUGHNUTS)

MAKES 3 DOZEN

In 2015, when I was just starting my reporting on subsistence food and climate change, I decided to make a trip to Point Hope to attend the whaling feast. I thought I'd set up a place to stay, but then it fell through at the last minute. I had to get on the plane anyway, and I'll never forget landing, getting out of the plane on a foggy runway, and realizing I had no idea how I was going to get to town from the airport.

But soon someone offered me a ride. And then, soon after that, Aanauraq Lane, or "Aana," adopted me and the photographer I was traveling with, found us a place to stay, and invited us in to help her make doughnuts. I spent most of the rest of the trip in kitchens, making doughnuts and then helping with akutuq. I learned that one way into the history and culture of a small community is through the kitchen.

After that, I started to keep track of the places where I encountered doughnuts as I traveled across the Arctic region. Flour, sugar, and oil came to Alaska Native communities with contact. Doughnuts and fry bread were then adopted and adapted as Alaska Native traditional foods. They aren't all that healthy, but they are what celebrations taste like. The smell of them frying takes me back to many a village gym gathering.

¾ cup sugar

½ teaspoon salt

1 cup hot water

½ cup milk

1½ tablespoons dry yeast

2½ cups flour, plus more for dusting

2 tablespoons butter, melted

2 eggs, beaten stiff

Zest of 1 lemon

½ teaspoon ground nutmeg

About 48 ounces oil, preferably peanut or vegetable

Optional: Sugar and cinnamon, for coating

In fact, one of the things I like about the many recipes that I've found in historic cookbooks and been given by readers on Facebook is that they are always for a lot of doughnuts, like eighty or one hundred. When you fry, you fry for a crowd. Subsistence, the biggest influencing force in how we all eat up here, is about sharing. There's also some entrepreneurial spirit in there. Doughnut fryers are known to advertise on Facebook when they have a fresh batch.

The hardest part about the recipe is getting the frying right. Doughnut-making is so second-nature to the people who write most of the recipes that there is usually no detail about how to fry. For novices, it's much easier if you use a candy thermometer. If the doughnuts are getting brown on the outside super quickly, like within twenty seconds, your oil is too hot. Alternately, if they don't get pretty close to done on one side after a minute, your oil isn't at temperature. (I burned many in the process of making mine without a thermometer.) Oh, and if you're a newbie, don't forget to put the fan on high and keep a fire extinguisher nearby. Chopsticks, which I first saw being used to fry doughnuts in Adak, are great for fishing them out of the oil.

This recipe for village-style doughnuts was adapted from King Cove Women's Club's *Our Favorite Recipes*, 1978. For the recipe, you will need a doughnut cutter and a candy thermometer.

In a large bowl, dissolve the sugar and salt in the hot water and the milk.
Sprinkle the yeast over the mixture and allow to dissolve, about 10 minutes.
Pour the mixture into a standing electric mixer with a paddle attachment
(or use a hand-held electric mixer with heavy-duty beaters). With the mixer
on medium speed, add the flour slowly and mix thoroughly. Pour in the
butter, eggs, lemon zest, and nutmeg.

Scrape the dough out onto a lightly floured work surface and knead, adding
a little additional flour when the dough is sticky, until the dough ball is firm
and only slightly sticky. Allow the dough to rise in a warm place for 2 hours.
Meanwhile, if you want to coat the doughnuts with sugar and cinnamon,
put a mixture of half sugar and half cinnamon in a small shallow bowl for
dipping.

Once the dough has risen, gently roll it on a floured surface and cut into
desired shapes. (If you don't have a doughnut cutter, use a glass and punch
a hole in the center with your finger.) Allow the doughnuts to rise for 20 to
30 minutes.

Meanwhile, fill a large Dutch oven or heavy pot about one-third full with
the oil. Heat the oil over medium heat to approximately 365°F. (If you don't
have a candy thermometer, you can tell the oil is hot and ready by throwing a popcorn kernel in. It should pop right away.) Fry the doughnuts in
batches, 1 to 2 minutes per side, until golden, turning with tongs or chopsticks. If desired, immediately roll each doughnut in the cinnamon-sugar
mixture.

RECIPE LIST

ACKNOWLEDGMENTS

Many thanks to:

Visual journalist collaborators Katie Orlinsky, Nathaniel Wilder, Joshua Corbett, Ash Adams, Anne Raup, Marc Lester, and Bob Hallinen.

The intrepid Jess Stugelmayer, who shot videos of the interviews in this book and always added one last great question.

Fine word editors, most especially Patrick Farrell at the *New York Times*, Katherine Lanpher from Al Jazeera America, Helen Rosner at Eater, and David Hulen, Vicky Ho, and Victoria Barber at the ADN.

Generous mentors Sam Sifton and Kim Severson, who helped me shape ideas, read my words, made them better, and believed I could do this. Ann Gerhart, who encouraged me to be ambitious.

The Pulitzer Center for Crisis Reporting for funding the travel that made my stories of rural Alaska possible.

Sara Boario, my forever friend, and my sweet extended family for helping to care for my boys so I could write and travel (especially His Pieness Uncle Tommy). Meg, my best pal. Kyle, for encouraging me to write recipes. Shiner Comics headquarters. Jack Carpenter, for all the editing songs.

Julie Decker, who made this book possible; brilliant Francesca DuBrock, who built its structure; and, above all, the many cooks, hunters, fisherpeople, and village subsistence experts, who have been my teachers.

CREDITS

Chapters and recipes have been revised and reprinted from their original publication in the following:

Chapter 1. In Alaska's Far-Flung Villages, Happiness is a Cake Mix. From *The New York Times*, September 18, 2017 © 2019 *The New York Times*. All rights reserved. Used by permission and protected by the copyright laws of the United States. The printing, copying, redistribution, or retransmission of this content without express written permission is prohibited.

Recipe: Dulce de Leche Poppy Seed Cake, author's own recipe.

Chapter 2. Whale Hunting at Point Hope, a Village Caught between Tradition and Climate Change. TheGuardian.com, July 16, 2015. Copyright Guardian News & Media Ltd 2018.

Recipe: Salmon Pot Pie with Parmesan Crust. Anchorage Daily News, September 20, 2018.

Chapter 3. Finding Produce in Alaska's Winters Takes Wiles and Luck. From *The New York Times*, February 21, 2018 © 2018 *The New York Times*. All rights reserved. Used by permission and protected by the copyright laws of the United States. The printing, copying, redistribution, or retransmission of this content without express written permission is prohibited.

Recipe: The Alaska Cocktail. Anchorage Daily News, June 21, 2018.

Chapter 4. Alaska Sprouts: The Future of Food Sprouts in Deep Winter. Edible Alaska, March 6, 2017.

Recipe: Sourdough Starter and Sourdough Pancakes. Sourdough Pancakes: *Anchorage Daily News,* June 27, 2018.

Chapter 5. In a City of Strip Malls, a Vietnamese Noodle Revolution. Anchorage Daily News, April 6, 2014.

Recipe: Foolproof Wild Blueberry Pie. Anchorage Daily News, August 30, 2018.

Chapter 6. Free Alaskan Salmon: Just Bring a Net and Expect a Crowd. From *The New York Times,* August 9, 2017 © 2019 *The New York Times.* All rights reserved. Used by permission and protected by the copyright laws of the United States. The printing, copying, redistribution, or retransmission of this content without express written permission is prohibited.

Recipe: Build Your Own "Secret" Salmon Spread. Anchorage Daily News, July 20, 2018.

Chapter 7. How Spam Musubi Edged Its Way into Anchorage's Food Scene. Anchorage Daily News, September 28, 2018.

Recipe: Spam Musubi and Musubi McMuffin. Anchorage Daily News, September 28, 2018.

Chapter 8. Thirty Days of Muktuk. Edible Alaska, November 9, 2017.

Recipe: Halibut Olympia. Anchorage Daily News, July 12, 2018.

Chapter 9. Eating Well at the End of the Road. Eater, October 15, 2014, https://www.eater.com/2014/10/15/6971503/homer-alaska. Used by permission from the writer, Eater, and Vox Media, Inc.

Recipe: Easy Alley Raspberry Jam, author's own recipe. Anchorage Daily News, August 2, 2018.

Chapter 10. Thousands of Miles from Washington, DC, the Gwich'in Track the Fate of Caribou Country. Al Jazeera America, March 14, 2015.

Recipe: Sort of Sarah Palin's Famous Moose Chili. Anchorage Daily News, October 18, 2018.

Afterword. Doughnuts at the Edge of the World. First published in *Alaska Magazine,* September, 2015.

Recipe: Village-Style Doughnuts (Sunshine Doughnuts). Anchorage Daily News, October 11, 2018.

PHOTOGRAPHY CREDITS

Photographs are listed by page number.

ABOUT THE AUTHOR

Julia O'Malley, a third-generation Alaskan, is an Anchorage-based food journalist. She writes recipes for the *Anchorage Daily News* and is a regular contributor to *Edible Alaska*. She was the Atwood Chair of Journalism at the University of Alaska Anchorage from 2015 to 2017 and now teaches writing workshops around the state. She has written about food, climate, and culture for *The Guardian*, Eater, *National Geographic*, *High Country News*, the *Washington Post*, and the *New York Times*, among other publications. She won a James Beard Award in 2018 in the foodways category. Her winning story about subsistence whale hunting in the Siberian Yupik village of Gambell was included in *The Best American Food Writing 2018*.

This book was published in collaboration with the Anchorage Museum to accompany an exhibition and series of public programs on Alaska's food culture. You can find more information about Julia's work at juliaomalley.media.

ABOUT ALASKA'S FOOD CULTURE

The Anchorage Museum is devoted to celebrating and preserving the stories of our place and time, the concepts that bind our communities, and the activities that express our humanity. The experiences of indigenous people in Alaska are intricately linked to the landscape and the sustenance of this place. Recent arrivals add new stories. In searching for ways to highlight environment, lifeways, and knowledge, food becomes a common theme, for the way it so clearly highlights the natural world and the ways that bond us as humans.

In Alaska, we have extreme landscapes, and vastly different ones as we move across the state, from rain forests to deserts to urban settlements to tundra and to the Arctic. These landscapes shape the food we harvest, grow, and preserve, and affect what we import and the ways we combine the new with what has existed since the beginning. Newcomers bring traditions and flavors from other places, and those mix with what is distinctly local. In that mix, we find our conversations—the stories of time and place. In that mix, we find the recipes that bring us together.

JULIE DECKER
Director and CEO
Anchorage Museum

Design by Katrina Noble
Composed in NCT Granite, typeface designed by Nathan Zimet
Map of Alaska by Ani Rucki

23   22   21   20   19   5   4   3   2   1

Printed and bound in the United States of America

UNIVERSITY OF WASHINGTON PRESS
uwapress.uw.edu

LIBRARY OF CONGRESS CATALOGING-IN-PUBLICATION DATA
Names: O'Malley, Julia, author. | Severson, Kim, other.
Title: The whale and the cupcake : stories of subsistence, longing, and community
    in Alaska / Julia O'Malley, Kim Severson.
Description: 1st edition. | Seattle : University of Washington Press, 2019.
Identifiers: LCCN 2019023559 (print) | LCCN 2019023560 (ebook) | ISBN 9780295746142
    (paperback) | ISBN 9780295746753 (epub)
Subjects: LCSH: Cooking, American. | Cooking—Alaska. | LCGFT: Cookbooks.
Classification: LCC TX715 .O51244 2019 (print) | LCC TX715 (ebook) | DDC 641.5973—dc23
LC record available at https://lccn.loc.gov/2019023559
LC ebook record available at https://lccn.loc.gov/2019023560